David Emery's

FULL
METAL
CARDIGAN

Adventures on the Frontline of Social Work

Full Metal Cardigan
David Emery

Published by Fledgling Press, 2018
Cover Design: Graeme Clarke
graeme@graemeclarke.co.uk

Print ISBN 9781912280179
eBook ISBN 9781912280186

www.fledglingpress.co.uk

Printed by MBM Print SCS Ltd

MIX
Paper from
responsible sources
FSC® C117931

To the NHS

FOREWORD

"To describe me as a user of social services is like calling a rat a user of Rentokil." Joanna

Service user, patient, client, customer, consumer, survivor, expert with experience. The list of labels given to the people I have worked with is long. They change with time, setting, location and context. A new one is coined, fresh and positive. Eventually it becomes steeped in stigma and is discarded. By some. Others stick with it. Last week, social services referred their client who, once accepted to our team, became a service user and, on further review by the doctor, a patient. He was found not to meet the eligibility criteria; he was a survivor but not with the right symptoms, an expert but with the wrong experience. He was promptly discharged and ended the day as just a person.

I have tried to avoid labels throughout the book but apologise when this has not been possible.

People's names, genders, ages, ethnicities, star signs, blood groups and positioning on the space-time continuum have been changed to protect their confidentiality (and my registration).

Everything else is true.

The police sergeant lowered his machine gun.

"We've shut down all of the surrounding streets but need this finished before the school run starts. Have you got the warrant?"

I pulled a tattered piece of paper from my pocket; the fruit of a three hour wait in court. Initially the magistrate had been reluctant to authorise it but, on learning the address was around the corner from his daughter's piccolo teacher, he was more forthcoming.

The sergeant checked it through. "Right then, let's go."

I slowly walked up to the bungalow, flanked by four armed officers; them in Kevlar bulletproof vests, me in a wool-mix cardigan.

Derick stood at the window, staring out impassively. The last time he had become this unwell it had ended with him chasing his elderly neighbours around their house with a knife in his hand and a fountain of blood pumping from his radial artery.

He thought they were members of the Illuminati.

They said that they hadn't even been to Wales.

Eventually I reached the door and prepared to deploy my trusted sponge knock, developed over years of not wanting to be heard.

Morning calls to crack dens, lunchtime visits to houses of poo, evening appointments with ASBO'd adolescents; my sponge knock had protected me from them all.

Taking a deep breath I gently wafted my knuckles against the door.

There was no answer.

God bless my sponge knock.

The police officers shifted impatiently behind me, desperate to kick the door in. This was something I wanted to avoid as it would not only stigmatise Derick further but would also require me to arrange the repair of the door once everyone else had gone home.

"Try again."

I tried again.

Nothing.

"Ok, step aside," said the sergeant and within seconds the door was forced and we were piling into his home.

As the dust settled I found myself face to face with Derick in his front room whilst the battalion of officers squeezed into the hallway behind.

I had no gun, no body armour and nowhere else to go.

Fighting hard to keep control of my emotions and my bowels, I pulled out the completed Mental Health Act section papers. These documents gave us the statutory right to be in his home, to remove him against his will, to forcibly convey him to hospital and to deprive him of his liberty. Our entire legal authority was conferred by these two pink forms.

Derick plucked them out of my hand and tore them up.

I lost control of my bowels a little bit.

ONE

Everyone else knew what they wanted to do. Adrian wanted to work with animals (he's now a butcher), Penny wanted to write poetry (she's on Jobseekers Allowance) and Kenneth wanted to be a vicar (prison). I had no such ambition and drifted through school without purpose, the only advice I received – don't be a teacher – coming from my dad (a teacher). I had presumed a plan would emerge at college but it never did. The one thing I did know was that I wanted to go to university. My sister had gone and I had seen how it had transformed her life. Before she had got her degree in psychology she had been a part-time counter assistant in a failing delicatessen; afterwards she was made full-time.

Having (just) achieved the grades I needed at college, I decided that I would study archaeology at university. This was partly because of the practical nature of the course, partly because of the high ratio of girls to boys the previous year, but mostly because of Indiana Jones. So great was my love of these films that I once convinced my mum to take me to the cinema to see the whole trilogy back-to-back, whereupon, after six and a half hours in the dark, I ran excitedly into the bright afternoon sunshine, promptly lost the use of my legs and had to be pushed all the way back to the car in a shopping trolley.

Upon starting my degree, I (and my entirely male class) grappled with the concept of self-motivated learning and how, if you didn't attend lectures, didn't read set texts, didn't submit essays and didn't sit exams, no one seemed to mind. With a knowledge of world chronology derived largely from children's television I (just) managed to scrape a second-class degree in archaeology and was handed a certificate, a trowel and responsibility for safeguarding the nation's ancient past.

It would not take long to realise that the life of an archaeologist was not for me. Alongside my extremely limited understanding of history (if it wasn't in Dogtanian and the Three Muskehounds it might as well not have happened), I proved to be completely inept at excavation. In my first week my sausage fingers managed to mangle an Iron Age bracelet resulting in the professor in charge of the dig postulating that a mighty slaughter had occurred on the site.

I knew better.

Worse was to follow when I failed to spot an important settlement boundary that I had been tasked with identifying. Wrongly assuming that the subtle change in soil colour was down to my plump colleague Alan's considerable shadow rather than a shift from manmade deposits to natural earth, I insisted that we continued to trowel, only coming to a standstill three days later when we struck the car park of Poundstretcher.

The travel and treasures that I had imagined as an undergraduate were never to materialise and, instead of ancient Egypt and Aztec gold, I was to spend six months of the year in a draughty portakabin scrubbing pottery fragments with a toothbrush. On one occasion I was flung out of a JCB scoop whilst trying to take an aerial photo of what I thought might be the markings of a Roman villa (they weren't – they were JCB tracks from the previous day) but, that aside, the general lack of adventure provided by a career in archaeology caused me to rethink my future.

Aware that I needed to do something different but unsure of what this might be, I was to persist in the portakabin until one fateful afternoon when, having been given the day off after traces of leptospirosis had been detected in the bones I had been handling for the last three months, I went down an alleyway in the local town and stumbled upon a volunteers' centre. Though I'd spent many lunchbreaks aimlessly wandering these streets, I had never noticed this before and, seeing it as a sign of the universe's cosmic intervention into my destiny (rather than my poor sense of direction), I decided to go in.

Inside, a smell of incense hung in the air and the mating calls of pregnant dolphins were being piped through antiquated speakers. In the far corner sat a wise crone with a scarf on her head, an amulet around her neck and a menthol cigarette in her hand.

"Come closer my dear," she beckoned, "come closer."

I sat down in front of her and, encouraged by her gentle coaxing, I told her about my need for change, to find something different, a fresh path to follow, a new adventure to begin. I was shocked by the strength of my own emotions as I poured my heart out to this stranger.

I would try anything.

Anything.

Anything.

After an hour, it was clear that anything did not include children, animals, old people, religion, nature, charity shops, public speaking, fundraising, horticulture, promotion, art, culture, heritage, stewarding or meals on wheels.

"That doesn't leave us with much," she told me, "except..."

Looking cautiously over her shoulder (which was odd as she had her back to the wall) she reached under her desk.

"Call this number," she whispered, passing me a tattered piece of card and disappearing into a fog of National Trust pamphlets.

Later that day I nervously called the number on the card.

Rob answered.

After establishing that I did not want my duvet cleaning (the team were based over a launderette and used the same phone line), he explained that he was a newly-qualified social worker who ran a group which gave young people with a learning disability the chance to go out socially. For many of its members, who attended centres or stayed at home during the day, the group was their only opportunity to go out with friends and Rob was passionate for it to work. Unlike more traditional, paternal services, the group was run as a collective and members were encouraged to vote for what they wanted to do each week. At the start of every meeting Rob would produce a list of diverse and stimulating activities that he had lovingly drawn up, only for them to be swiftly rejected in favour of a night at McDonalds.

Every week.

Rob told me that his main challenge (other than not contracting rickets after countless Happy Meals) was retaining the volunteers who all tended to leave after the first week, never to return again.

I asked him why this was.

He said he wasn't sure but thought it may be linked to the long hours, high risk, poor resources, no pay, lack of recognition, and could I start that evening?

I laughed.

He laughed.

We both laughed.

Until I realised that he was serious.

"I'm going to have to think about it," I said, unable to think of an excuse fast enough.

An hour later I stood in the train station carpark, looking out for Rob and still unable to think of an excuse. When he finally arrived, he put my preconceived ideas of what a social worker would look like to shame.

I had envisaged someone with a beard, brogues and a beige woolly jumper.

I was wrong.

His woolly jumper was green.

"Have you ever done anything like this before?" he asked, as we waited for the others.

As my only previous work experience had been in a café where two of my egg and cress sandwiches were returned because they contained soil and a builder had once started to weep because I blew my nose whilst making his bacon roll, it was clear that I had not done anything remotely like this before.

"Yes," I was surprised to hear myself reply.

"Good, when everyone's here we'll split them into two groups and we can take one each."

"But how many people will there be?" I asked, a note of panic in my voice.

"No idea," he replied confidently.

Over the next hour people started to arrive, dropped off by exhausted family, friends and carers who would then screech off, anxious to squeeze every second out of the short respite the group provided them with. Before long, Rob and I were engulfed by a crowd of excited young people, laughing, joking and making hurtful comments about the pea green tracksuit bottoms that I had foolishly chosen to wear in an attempt to be down with the kids.

"Ok,'" said Rob eventually, "I think that's everyone. Why don't you take that half and I'll take the other?"

He bisected the group with an outstretched arm.

"That's a lot of people," I said surveying the jostling throng in front of me.

"But you'll have Nicci helping you," said Rob, reassuringly, "I wouldn't expect you to do it on your own on your first night."

This came as something of a relief as it would only be the second time in my life that I had had to look after someone who wasn't me – the other time was when I was asked to keep an eye on my three-year-old niece at a family wedding.

Midway through the buffet she had come up to me and handed me a sausage roll.

"Thank you very much," I said, before realising it was, in fact, a poo.

When Nicci appeared, she was not an experienced elder

who could shower me with wisdom and guide me through the intricacies of human behaviour. Nor was she a nubile young student I could bond with on this intimate voyage of discovery. Nicci was Nicholas, the eight-year-old little brother of one of the group members.

"Hello," he said, waving his Teenage Mutant Ninja Turtle at me (Ronaldo, I think).

I looked pleadingly at Rob.

"I think we should go now," he said quickly, sensing that he might be about to lose another volunteer.

The short walk from the carpark to the platform nearly killed me. Issuing a string of feeble commands that were heard by all and heeded by none, I tried my best, but soon realised that my ability to manage the group effectively was severely compromised by being unsure of people's names.

"Lucy, stop dangling John off the edge of the platform!" I shouted frantically.

"That's not Lucy, that's Lisa," corrected Nicholas.

"Lisa, stop dangling John off the edge of the platform!" I shouted frantically.

"That's not John, that's Phil."

I saw danger everywhere. The live tracks, the speeding railway stock, the plastic flap on the ticket machine. I had previously seen myself as a carefree, happy-go-lucky risk taker. At university, my cavalier lifestyle had resulted in more visits to A&E than anyone else, from a splinter in my scrotum when sliding naked down a bannister, to falling off a bridge with a girl on my shoulders who, just moments earlier, had confided in me she had a fear of both heights and water. Yet here I was, a gibbering wreck in jazzy sweatpants.

Miraculously, and with only one significant injury

(Ronaldo was decapitated by the plastic flap of the ticket machine), my group eventually made it onto the train and, as we set off towards the city centre, I started to relax and enjoy the company of the young people around me.

Unfortunately this was not to last long.

As the train prepared to leave a station, young Bobby, a boy who appeared to share my passion for Raiders of the Lost Ark, suddenly jumped up from his chair, ran the length of the carriage and dived through the rapidly closing doors. They slammed shut behind him, missing his built-up shoe by millimetres, and, before I had a chance to react, the train pulled away.

"Bobby!" I cried, my nose pressed against the window, as he (and my future career in social work) disappeared into the distance, "Booobbbbyyy!!!"

Nicholas came and patted me gently on the back.

"That was actually Greg," he whispered.

Eventually, after a desperate manhunt across the railway network, we were able to track down Greg (who was sipping from a homeless man's can of Irn Bru) and resume our evening (at McDonalds). But such a near miss was not an isolated incident, and over subsequent weeks we would regularly lose vulnerable young people in bus terminals, shopping precincts, red-light districts and military firing ranges throughout the city. Yet by 11pm we would all, somehow, have made it back to the station carpark with family, friends and carers waiting to collect their charges, blissfully unaware of the night's events.

TWO

Over time, the feeling of terror that preceded every trip out with the group turned to one of enjoyment and I soon found myself looking forward to the evenings rather than dreading them. I gradually got to know all of the members and loved the energy and enthusiasm that they brought with them each week. I got used to the many demands of the role and how best to manage them. I learned how to give off an air of calm when inside I flapped, how to ignore the disgruntled mumblings of members of the public whose train carriage we had invaded, and how to ensure that I was always further away than Rob when someone's toileting accident needed to be addressed.

Whilst I continued to spend my days buffing up the bones of the dead, I knew in my heart that I wanted to work with the living. With large debts and unpaid rent, I had intended to embark upon a career change in a measured, planned way but, on being presented with another box of filthy clavicles one Thursday morning, I decided that I could not face it anymore and downed my toothbrush and trowel for good.

By now my sister, having lopped off two of her fingertips whilst slicing garlic sausage, had left the delicatessen and started to work for a charity that supported people with a learning disability to live in the community. The homes were located within leafy villages and were always advertising for staff. My sister encouraged me to apply and after a brief interview, in which I was asked my name and if I had any (really bad) criminal convictions, I was offered night shifts in one of the homes.

In which one was it to be? I speculated.

Sunny Meadows?

Honeysuckle Cottage?

Mulberry Farm?

No. Grimethorpe House, smack in the middle of the largest council estate in Europe.

As I drove to the house on my first day of work, I spotted a group of children sat talking on the kerb. Full of positive energy and joie de vivre, I slowed down and bid them a good day.

They pelted my car with grit.

I pulled over to the side of the road and marched angrily towards them, expecting them to flee.

They stood and stared. One put out his cigarette. Another screwed the top back on her bottle of gin. I stopped, untied my shoelace, tied my shoelace, walked back to my car and drove off.

I'd made my point.

The home I would be working in was for three men, Roger, Kamal and Michael who all had challenging behaviour. New to the profession and its accompanying terminology, I assumed this to mean that they would be engaging me in controversial philosophical debates or airing provocative political views. Unfortunately it turned out to be more along the lines of throwing casserole dishes across the kitchen and trying to bite me when Top Gear finished.

After the briefest of inductions from an exhausted

colleague (there's the tea, there's the coffee and there's the adrenaline shot that you might need to stop someone dying from anaphylactic shock), I was asked to start doing shifts on my own. In the early weeks, sleep proved elusive and I would lie awake listening for any disturbances. On this estate disturbances were not uncommon with the sound of dogs, motor bikes and semi-automatic weapons echoing into the evening air. Eventually though, as I got to know the home and the people who lived in it, I became more relaxed and would sometimes get a full eight minutes' sleep before I was awoken by the unmistakable thud of a surface-to-air missile being launched out of the next-door neighbour's garden.

During the day the three residents attended a local centre and so I was required to work frantically in the morning to get them ready for the minibus and meet them when they got home to help them get changed, have dinner, relax and go to bed. In-between those times I would rock backwards and forwards in the foetal position in a darkened room. The minibus arrived at 8am sharp and the driver, a fearsome slab of a man on a tight schedule, would always aggressively ring the door bell (no mean feat when it played a glockenspiel rendition of The Sun Has Got His Hat On) until I brought the residents out.

One morning I woke to find that I had overslept.

It was 7.30am.

I usually got up at 5.30am.

I hurriedly pulled on my trousers and t-shirt and burst into Roger's room only to find him munching upon his own poo. This came as something of a shock, not least because he had refused a pork chop I had made him the previous day. I backed out and gathered myself on the landing, quickly realising that I was going to have to sort this out myself. I grabbed a toothbrush and put the radio on. Mark Morrison was playing and I started to brush.

It was like being back in the portakabin.

As we stood face to face, Roger and I harmonised to Return of the Mack whilst I discreetly turned around and dry-retched at the end of each chorus.

After this incident I would not sleep soundly again as my ears strained for the sound of thrutching bowels in the night.

I would also never enjoy listening to Mark Morrison.

(In supervision, some weeks later, I told my manager about this and she recounted how, when Roger's dad had dropped him off on his first day at the home, she had asked him if there was anything they needed to know.

"Let's just say he enjoys breakfast in bed," he had cryptically replied.)

My problems with sleep were to become even more pronounced when my colleague Lisa, on completing a handover to me at the end of her shift, dropped a bombshell.

"The medication's been ordered, there's chops for dinner and Kamal's birthday cake is in the fridge. Oh, and Nana Ogden was at it again last night."

She picked up her handbag and went to leave.

"Nana Ogden?" I inquired.

"Yes, for hours. Wouldn't stop."

"Who's Nana Ogden?"

"No one's told you about Nana Ogden?"

Since starting there no one had told me how to use the phone, where the toilets were or how to avoid being hit by a flying Le Creuset lid, never mind who Nana Ogden was.

"Oh God," she said, sitting down and put her hand on mine, "I just assumed…"

Nana Ogden, it transpired, was a ghostly apparition who wandered the house at night, only visible in the many mirrors that covered the walls (an odd choice, I thought, to put up lots of mirrors when you had a mirror-loving spectral-being in residence). She had been held responsible for fire alarms going off, windows being opened, objects being moved and several staff resignations.

"And she hates men," finished Lisa.

We sat in silence.

Lisa patted my shoulder.

At least I was not alone.

"Christ!" she said suddenly, "I'm going to miss my bus! Bye!"

I was alone.

I had a complicated relationship with ghosts. My mum had died when I was young and so part of me wanted to see one as proof of an afterlife that I really didn't believe in. But an incident at Cub camp where something icy had rubbed against my thigh during the night (though Graham, who lay in the sleeping bag next to me and whose civil partnership I recently attended, saw nothing) had put me right off. In my heart, I wanted to see Nana Ogden but in my head I was terrified.

After Lisa's revelation I spent the whole of that evening clutching a biography of Cliff Richards (there was no Bible in the house) and averting my gaze from any reflective surfaces. After hurriedly getting the residents to bed I hunkered down in the office, my eyes fixed on the door, quietly reciting the Lord's Prayer under my breath. I was just drifting off when I heard a loud banging from downstairs. I tried my best to ignore it but it persisted.

Eventually I decided that I must face whatever was

waiting for me. I picked up a can of Lynx deodorant and went downstairs.

The noise was coming from the kitchen and so, edging towards the door, I nervously turned on the light and peered in.

It took a moment for my eyes to adjust but then I saw it; a dark shadowy figure by the fridge being reflected in the window.

I shrieked.

This was the moment, I realised, when my refusal to acknowledge the possibility of the paranormal would be punished. Holding the Lynx in front of me I went in, prepared to face this vengeful wraith (and give it a good spraying of Congo Mist).

But it wasn't a vengeful wraith.

It was Roger.

After gently bringing an end to his midnight feast I helped him to his bedroom and went back to the kitchen to tidy up. I opened the fridge to put the butter back.

I shrieked again.

A malevolent face was peering out of Kamal's birthday cake.

Nana Ogden.

I ran back to the office and barricaded myself in.

The next morning, deprived of all sleep, I stumbled out of my room and tiptoed downstairs to confront the cake. With the sun shining and my glasses on, I was able to undertake a comprehensive examination and it soon became clear that this was not the supernatural mark of Nana Ogden in the buttercream icing.

It was Roger again.

The greedy little sod must have sunk his face into the

cake last night and left an imprint so clear that, if I'd poured plaster over it and allowed it to set (like the FBI do with a serial killer's footprints) I would have been able to pull off his perfect death mask.

Now that I was a fully (if meagrely) paid member of staff I was required to attend regular mandatory training sessions provided by the organisation, to equip me with the skills needed to practice safely (and, coincidentally, give them legal protection from criminal negligence). Fire safety, first aid, food hygiene: all delivered on an annual basis and, though I have attended them countless times, I still don't know which colour extinguisher will put out an electrical fire, how many chest compressions to give someone in cardiac arrest or where to put a chicken in the fridge. I've probably spent more time learning how to clean shellfish properly than spot signs of abuse in children. New levels of uselessness were set by a moving and handling course that I completed over the internet and an infection control course delivered by a man with filthy fingers.

One of the most relevant courses that I attended during this time was epilepsy awareness because Kamal and Michael both had seizures. During the course the facilitator went through a list of do's and don'ts:

"And obviously," she said, shaking her head, "you should never give someone a drink of water when they are having a seizure."

We all scoffed at such a preposterous idea.

It was several months later when, awoken by the sounds of a person in distress at 3am, I stumbled into a resident's room to find them having a seizure.

I tried to summon up my training.

"And obviously," I remembered through a foggy haze, "you should always give someone a drink of water when they are having a seizure."

I rushed to the bathroom and filled up a large jug with water. As I bent over Michael, ready to pour several litres of liquid down his gullet, his eyes widened in horror and his seizure came to an abrupt end.

Fear of a water-boarding had brought him out of a grand mal.

It would not be long, however, before Michael paid me back for this incident.

Michael suffered from involuntary verbal ticks including a number of phrases he would often repeat.

It's all gone wrong, hello, hello and she's sexy! were a few of his favourites.

One morning I was sitting with him in a packed doctor's waiting room when Michael pointed to a poster on the wall.

"She's sexy!" he boomed, "she's sexy!"

The other patients smiled warmly at him and turned to see the poster.

It was a new-born baby having an injection.

THREE

A move south, inspired by love, adventure and a wish to escape an alcoholic, one-and-a-half-eared line manager, meant that I had to leave my job at Grimethorpe House after only a year. Despite the low pay, sleep deprivation and faecal petit déjeuners, my time with Roger, Kamal, Michael and Nana O (as I had affectionately come to know her) had confirmed my passion for this work and I knew it was something I wanted to continue. Luckily the charity that had employed me was a national one and I was able to apply for a job at another of their properties with relative ease.

The new home was much larger, housing nine people and, after attending a short interview, I was given the news that I had been successful. Susan, a resident who had been on the interview panel, confirmed my appointment by informing me that she would now name one of her goldfish after me. This was a long-standing tradition in the home and so, later that evening, one fish went to sleep as Helga (whose Norwegian namesake had made a swift departure after a number of sex lines had showed up on the phone bill) and was reborn the next day as David.

It was 5am, several weeks later when there was a violent banging on the door of the office.

"Betty's dead! Betty's dead! Betty's dead!"

I jumped up from a deep sleep and stumbled around in a daze, answering phones that weren't ringing and turning off alarms that were silent. Eventually I put my clothes on (backwards) and opened the door.

Susan stood there in her pyjamas and steamed-up glasses.

Her hearing aids whistled.

"Terrible news," she said holding out her hand to me, "Betty's…"

"Dead?" I ventured.

I looked down to see a distressed goldfish flipping around on her palm. It quickly became clear that whilst Betty the goldfish may indeed be dead, Tony, whom Susan had mistakenly hooked out of her filthy tank, wasn't. I grabbed poor Tony, rushed him back to the tank and threw him in.

He plopped gratefully back into the water.

Betty, who did not look quite so joyful, floated lifelessly on the surface. Using a fish slice and a copy of Women's Weekly I solemnly scooped her out and buried her in the garden with the countless other pet corpses.

Susan had a heart of gold but the mothering instincts of Genghis Khan.

Living alongside Susan were eight other people and Pebbles the cat. Obese and toothless, Pebbles spent her days moving from lap to lap, waiting for a new staff member to start a shift so that she could hoodwink them into giving her another bowl of food.

"Pebbles is so good for them," commented a colleague one day as we sat watching Edith lovingly stroke her.

It was only when Pebbles came into the room that we

realised that Edith had been petting a bobble hat for the last ten minutes.

Pebbles' nemesis was a nameless, scraggy white stray that wandered in from time to time. Starved and full of fleas, he would nervously creep into the house, hopeful that a few drops of the love poured onto Pebbles would fall his way.

It never did.

On spotting the intruder a cry would go up and the residents (many of whom were reliant on walking aids) would spring to their feet and chase him off. Vile curses and bits of soil would be thrown at the wretched animal before everyone went back to their jigsaws so that their adrenaline levels could settle.

Every Friday at the home we would have a team meeting to discuss any issues that had arisen the previous week: faulty washing machines, the wrong brand of cereal, updates on the hanging baskets and, time permitting, the lives of the residents. Once a month we would be joined by Joy, a clinical psychologist, who would offer suggestions and interpretations on some of the problems we faced. These were often invaluable and allowed us to consider the psychological needs of the residents in greater depth. With Joy's help we were able to develop effective care plans to manage self-harm, obsessive rituals and low self-esteem.

Sometimes, however, I felt things went too far.

When an ongoing strong smell of urine was found to be coming from the corner of Edward's room, Joy excitedly told us about the aggression of this act and its significance in denoting ownership. Within the blink of an eye poor

Edward was whisked into weekly one-to-one sessions to improve his sense of citizenship and to emphasise the need for more appropriate forms of communication. It would only be several years later that a carpet fitter found that a leaking waste pipe was the cause of the stink, rather than Edward's psychological distress.

Another time, the home was hit with a spate of toilet rolls being jammed down the toilet, causing flooding, stench and expensive visits from the emergency plumber.

We had no idea who was responsible.

Joy did.

"It's clearly Trevor," she said, singling out a gentle, older resident who had recently been diagnosed with early onset dementia. "At some nonverbal level he is trying to tell us that the home is no longer meeting his needs."

Trevor was swiftly transferred to a more intensely staffed nursing home and we all felt satisfied with the outcome – that is until we overheard Alastair confessing to his sister over the phone that he had been responsible for the bog blocking so that he could get his hands on Trevor's larger, en-suite bedroom.

Joy's final pièce de résistance was when she facilitated our team building day, the centrepiece of which was an exercise she had devised in which we all had to say one thing we didn't like about each of our colleagues. After an hour of accusations and recriminations about weeing on the toilet seat, leaving out-of-date yogurt in the fridge and who was responsible for the stains on the sleepover bed (me), the team were able to come together as one and bond over the decision to pull Joy's plug for good.

*

Around this time I was introduced to the benefits system and learned how to ensure that the people I supported were receiving the money that they were entitled to. The system was incredibly complex but luckily, a local authority agency, the Money Advice Unit, was always on hand to help. As well as providing training sessions they also ran a telephone helpline that I used on a regular basis and so, when I received an ominous letter from the Department of Work and Pensions saying that they had overpaid a resident by £12,000 over the last ten years, I reached for the phone.

After giving my name and place of work, the advisor told me about the relationship between Housing Benefit and Income Support and how the award of Severe Disability Allowance could reduce the former and be means-tested against the latter. I quickly gave up trying to follow her and decided that this was a matter I could pass up to my manager.

"Now," said the advisor, unaware of my flagging attention, "you need to formally challenge their decision and quote the following piece of case law. Have you got a pen and paper?"

"Yes," I lied, putting my feet on the table with no thoughts of either pen or paper.

"Write down that in the ruling of B.W. vs Secretary of State."

"B...W...vs..." I repeated theatrically, not writing a thing.

"That a person who lacks capacity."

"Lacks...hang on...capacity..." I said, getting more elaborate with my deception.

"Could be deemed."

"Be...deemed..."

And so we went on for the next ten minutes.

Finally, she reached the end.

"With no potential for recourse."

"Po...ten...tial...for...re...course," I finished with a flourish.

"Now," she said, "read that back to me."

"..."

"Hello?"

"..."

"Hello?"

"Hello," I whimpered eventually.

"Could you read that back to me?"

I desperately wracked my brains for a way out but none was forthcoming. Honesty was the best policy but not always the one I chose.

I put the phone down, ashamed, and never called them again.

The highlight of the year for the residents was the summer holiday. Setting off at three in the morning, our convoy of two Volkswagen Polos and a Nissan Bongo would arrive at our destination after dark, having had to stop (thanks to Edith's dicky bladder) at every service station, lay-by and bushy thicket we passed. Tense and exhausted, the following hours would then be spent wandering the pitch-black campsite looking for our rooms whilst ruffians fought and fornicated around us.

With six of us to each tiny chalet, I would have to spend the next week in close proximity to Tony, who started each day by eating a pickled onion as a homeopathic remedy for his hay fever. The ensuing pong would ensure that pollen (and all of the other holidaymakers) stayed well away. The beds we were provided with were tiny, flimsy things and we would have to negotiate which way we would lie in order to all fit in. With Tony's bottom inches from my head it felt less like a holiday and more Das Boot. The doors were like paper and, in the early hours of day five, deprived of sleep and half-insane from Edith's relentless snoring, I found myself building a barricade out of cool boxes and empty pickled onion jars to try and dampen the noise.

The ensuing week would be spent going on trips during the day and discos at night. The destinations of the day trips would become increasingly desperate as the holiday progressed and options became more limited. We would start by going to local farms and candle factories and by the end of the week we would be pushing wheelchairs up mountains to see the sparse ruins of an ancient horse trough.

Each evening we would return to the holiday camp and go through the bundles of leaflets and maps in search of inspiration for the next day's events.

One night I saw we were several hours away from the town of Frampton. This was a town I knew well but couldn't quite place why. There must be something there, most likely from my archaeology days, I reasoned. It was only after our three cars had pulled into the deserted town centre that I remembered why I knew it: the girl that I had dropped off the bridge at university had come from there. Tony, who had had to endure two hours in a stuffy Nissan Bongo, listening to Edith wax lyrical about her sister's inability to conceive, was not impressed.

In the evenings we would gather at the social club for the disco. As the staff stood around watching the residents dance, I would think about some of the Disability Living Applications I had completed for the people in front of me.

Only days earlier I had completed a report for the benefits agency to confirm that Daniel struggled to walk ten yards unaided and here he was moonwalking to Smooth Criminal. Whilst Jen harmonised to Charles and Eddie in the centre of the dance-floor she received £72.90 a week care component for her social anxiety.

Would I lie to you baby, would I lie to you?

Apparently so.

The grand finale for the week was a celebrity cabaret but by the time that this arrived I was so exhausted I was hallucinating and had no interest in seeing a Gary Glitter tribute band, a Rolf Harris impersonator or, worse still, Simply Red.

Together with holidays, birthdays were also an important event in the home's calendar and, months before his fiftieth birthday arrived, Alastair was clear about what he was going to do for his: go-karting.

Alastair had not driven in over twenty years following his conviction for driving under the influence, although after the twelve pints of strong lager that were found in his system it was less an influence, more a decree. He loved motor sports and I was keen to get him back behind the wheel, and so I booked places for all the residents and two staff members, Gary and I, at the local indoor track.

On a cold Saturday morning we arrived en masse and went into the driver's centre. It was only when I saw them helping Edith to put down her walking stick and step into a flameproof bodysuit that I started to question the appropriateness of the activity. But Alastair's excitement carried me along and before long we were all standing trackside in helmets and neck braces.

"This," said the race coordinator with a flourish, "is what you'll be driving."

He pointed towards a fleet of shiny high powered go-karts and, despite my helmet, hood and noise defenders, I heard Gary gulp from across the track.

"Now, if we could all get in, I'll take you through the basics."

We clambered in and started to familiarise ourselves with the controls.

"These are two litre, twenty-eight horse power beasts that can go from 0 to 40 in six seconds," he said.

Or he had wanted to say.

Unfortunately, somewhere between these and are, Alastair had floored his pedal and wanged into the back of Gary at thirty miles an hour. Gary jolted forward, throwing up his hands like the shot soldier on the poster for Platoon. Others reflexively followed and all around me go-karts leapt briefly into life before tyre walls, hay bales and small children on a day out got in their way. A man stood in the track and furiously waved a red flag before diving over a safety bank as Hilary, an older woman with a significant visual impairment, hurtled towards him with the precision of a laser-guided missile.

*

Though I enjoyed these activities (usually after several months of psychotherapy), I started to become frustrated with the limitations of being a support worker. When Edith wanted to go to a new reminiscence group at the local day centre we were told that we would have to wait for a social worker to come and approve this. Months went by and Edith missed opportunity after opportunity to tell a captive audience about her barren sister. Eventually, a hairy youth appeared at our door and introduced himself as the social worker. After a few minutes of small talk he signed a form and Edith could go to the day centre. It was then and there that I decided I was going to train to be a social worker. Not only would it give me the means of empowering people and enable them to achieve greater levels of independence but, if someone in a Helloween t-shirt could do it, then so could I.

FOUR

To give myself a good chance of getting a place on a social work course, I knew that I needed to work in other fields of social care. The training was extremely competitive and a sandwich-making archaeologist with minimal relevant experience would struggle to be noticed amongst the support workers, psychology graduates and ex-offenders who traditionally applied to become social workers. I scoured the local papers for additional work I could do in the evenings but, without qualifications, I was limited to being a security guard or a male prostitute; neither of which would be good for my dicky knees. Eventually, after months of nothing, I stumbled upon an advert for a newly-created, one night a week, youth worker post. This seemed ideal as it would enable me to get the experience I needed whilst not having to give up my other job. I refined (fabricated) my CV and applied.

Several months later, long after I had forgotten about my application, I received an invite to a recruitment afternoon where a small group of us had to do a number of group activities whilst being observed by people with clipboards. After I had successfully managed to traverse the room with only a plant pot and a bit of dental floss, I was told that I had been successful and was invited for an induction the next evening with the other appointed candidates.

We were told the posts had been created in an attempt to

engage those young people who were disillusioned, at risk of abuse or, as seemed to be more common, causing bother outside a local councillor's house. Like a Navy Seal's task force, the five team members would be deployed at night to engage the children in more meaningful activities, other than sniffing glue or getting pregnant. We were solemnly handed an antiquated book on fun activities for young people and sent onto the mean streets of Middle England.

It later transpired that the five of us were the only people who had applied for the posts and, as we walked towards a large group of hoodies armed only with a copy of the team building game That's My Orange! it became clear why. The exercise was intended to encourage the development of communication and observation skills. The only thing it encouraged these hooligans to do was assault us with citrus fruit.

Although we managed to stick it out for over a year, it wasn't a job that any of us enjoyed and we finally decided enough was enough when, twelve months later on a cold winter's night, the five of us found ourselves crouching behind a postbox, desperately trying to hide from a passing group of children.

"I think they saw me," said Paula, terrified.

"Don't worry," said Shelly, "if they head this way we can run across the park."

Before that night was to come however, there would be some successes, many failures and the occasional incident of unspeakable betrayal.

One of the successes (for the children at least) was a day out at Laser Quest, though it was to prove less enjoyable for me. With a laser pack on my back, a gun in my hands and adrenaline coursing through my veins, I charged into the death zone battle arena only to go over on my ankle within minutes of the battle commencing. Aware that I had now become nothing more than cannon fodder, I feebly dragged myself to the side but was unable to avoid detection for long. Having spotted me quivering in a darkened corner, the merciless youngsters encircled me and spent the rest of the game racking up high scores by taking shots at my crumpled body.

One of our most spectacular failures occurred when we were asked to work alongside the bouncers of a newly-opened under-18s nightclub to ensure that the young people who attended had a safe and enjoyable evening. Struggling to decide what to wear, I arrived late and was told by the doorman that I should go straight into the main room. I opened the door expecting to find Agadoo and party poppers but instead was presented with a scene somewhere between Hieronymus Bosch and a Greco Roman orgy. Youths stumbled around, fighting or groping each other, whilst they downed spirits and snorted speed. I had eventually chosen to wear all black which, underneath the neon lights, gave me the appearance of a man with chronic dandruff; a man with chronic dandruff who, according to the number of wasted youths who came up to me to ask for a fiver of whiz, dealt drugs. After several hours, the smoke and music took its toll and, with six cans of isotonic Lucozade Sport coursing through my veins, I stumbled onto the main stage, tripped over a power cable and brought a dubstep sound clash to an abrupt halt.

As the crowd, annoyed at no longer being able to step to

the dub, started to bay for my blood, I decided that it was time to go home.

A young boy nodded to me at the door.

"Safe," he said holding out a clenched fist for a fist bump.

I shook it and went home.

Unspeakable betrayal was to take place in a small, rural village where we had been asked to work with a large group of bored children who were causing merry hell for the local residents. I already knew many of these children by sight because it was the same small, rural village that I had recently moved into and I often saw them playing football in the car park outside my house. Though I tended to avoid working where I lived, taking this job meant that I wouldn't have too far to travel and I might no longer be verbally abused each time I moved my Volkswagen goalpost.

We first met the main group of children at the village hall.

They were on the roof.

We shouted up to explain who we were and why we were there.

They listened politely before telling us to fuck off.

Undeterred, we kept going back and, after several weeks, we were able to build a rapport with some of them. They told us that their main interest was skateboarding but the only place that they were able to skate was on the pavements outside shops and people's houses. What they needed was a skateboard park so that they could enjoy themselves without bothering other people. I was impressed by their enthusiasm and so we agreed that we would take on the ambitious plan of getting the village its own skateboard park.

The young people threw themselves into the task and before long we had collected a five hundred-name petition, made a badly edited documentary and attended the parish annual general meeting to present our proposals.

The next week I received a call from an employee of the council planning department. "I've been asked to take this skateboarding proposal forward and wondered whether we could meet up?"

I couldn't believe it.

After months of asking children what they wanted and promptly doing nothing about it, we finally had a result. I excitedly arranged to meet with the town planner the next day where he went through the proposal with me.

"We've identified an area of land owned by the council that would be ideal," he said, passing me a detailed plan of the area.

It took a moment to orientate myself to the map, but eventually the proposal became clear; the skateboard park would be directly behind my house.

As I stood there I thought of the pleasure that it would bring to the young people I had grown so fond of. Not only of the sheer joy of skateboarding in a safe, purpose-built facility away from people who didn't want you, but of the idea that through dedication and commitment they could affect change. And then I thought of those little fuckers banging and clanking all through the night, sniffing glue and getting pregnant.

I told him I would get back to him.

I never did and the project died a death.

And so did a part of me.

For a few minutes.

FIVE

Historically, alongside people with mental health problems and unmarried mothers, large numbers of people with a learning disability were placed in long-stay hospitals. Located in rural backwaters where property prices were cheap and children feared to tread, the hospitals were bleak, self-contained worlds in which the inhabitants often spent their whole lives having little contact with the rest of society. Though concerns about their appropriateness were raised in the early 1960s, these hospitals continued to be used until the 1990s when changes in public opinion and a growing political will saw a move towards care in the community which was more inclusive and less expensive. Whilst community care would clearly benefit those people who were to follow, for the generation who lived through the shift from institution to independence, it was often traumatic.

Bob, Alf, Frank and Norman were one such group of people who, one Tuesday afternoon in the 1980s, found themselves being unceremoniously ripped from a hospital they did not want to leave and plopped into a four-bedroomed council house they did not want to go to. Although they had each been allocated a social worker to oversee their move, pressures on local authority budgets meant that once they had unpacked their few belongings, arranged their benefits and set up a standing order to pay for their rent they were left to fend for themselves.

The charity that I worked for as a support worker had recently taken over the running of their home and I was asked if I would like to manage it. I already knew the men well as they were part of Edith's extensive surveillance network which kept a close eye on all of the comings and goings in the community, and I would regularly take her round so that she could gather the latest intel. The home (like its owners) was warm but dishevelled and I was excited about the opportunity to try and improve things. The move into management would also increase my chances of getting onto the social work course.

A colleague of mine, Lisa, had already worked with the men for many years and I got on well with her. I had first met her when she had accidentally got sozzled on alcopops during a group outing and I had had to go and collect her. She had spent the afternoon merrily drinking Hooch lemonade, unaware of its 5.2% alcohol content. When she had gone to stand up to drive the residents home she found that she couldn't.

When I accepted the job, I became Lisa's line manager and this gave me my first experience of supervising someone. I had always valued my own supervision as a means of reflecting upon my practice and developing my knowledge and skills. Lisa used it to discuss how she could have her ex-husband (and the much-adored father of her two young daughters) killed. In the beginning I would smile and ignore it but, over time, Lisa's fantasies took shape and when she excitedly told me about a man she had met in the pub who would whack her ex for three grand and a bottle of single malt whisky I politely requested that she kept it to herself.

The other issue that regularly came up in Lisa's

supervisions was Bob's infatuation with her. Initially I had downplayed it, stressing that it was normal behaviour and, as long as he remained respectful, then it was something we should acknowledge and work with.

"But haven't you seen the photos?" asked Lisa, exasperated after months of raising it with me and no action being taken.

I hadn't and so one afternoon when Bob was at the day centre I decided to investigate.

Cautiously pushing open the door, I entered Bob's bedroom. Inside was dark and musty, the thick, nicotine-coated net curtains blocking out most of the light. I peered around and noticed that the far wall was covered in photographs. I went to investigate and, as I got closer, I could see that Bob had created a spectacular collage of 1960s porn.

I pulled opened the curtains for a better view.

As the natural light flooded in my blood ran cold.

On each of the writhing pornstar's bodies, Lisa's head (cut from old Christmas photos and complete with paper hat on her head and a kazoo in her mouth) had been carefully spliced on. I stumbled out of the room and slammed the door shut. When Bob arrived home from the day centre I was waiting for him and by the next day all of Lisa's kazoo-blowing heads were in the recycling.

Bob's best friend was Alf. Alf was housebound through paranoia and spent his days watching Westerns and ordering useless things through mail order catalogues. An early pioneer of home shopping, I would spend much of the years to come sorting out financial scrapes that Alf had got himself into. Like Smaug the dragon, he would sit atop his pile of treasure, afraid to sleep in case anyone should try to steal a plate commemorating Princess Anne's 38th birthday. He was convinced that the government had put him under surveillance and would insist his front room was bugged.

"Look," I once said after he thought he'd seen a microchip under his Fistful of Dollars cushion, "nothing."

I lifted it up.

"What's that then?" he said, pointing to a microchip which, it was later discovered, had fallen out of a colleague's phone.

Alf came from Little 'amden (Hampden) and would tell anyone who would listen (and many who would not) about the wonders of Little 'amden. One of the first things I did on starting the job was to take Alf to Little 'amden where he proceeded to spend the whole weekend asking to go back home.

Because he was at home most of the time, Alf had taken charge of the household duties and so I met with him one morning to do my initial health and safety checks. As well as checking fire alarms, exit points and fridge temperatures, I had to go through all of the cleaning products with him.

"What's this used for?" I asked, holding up a large can of industrial detergent.

"Cleaning our glasses," said Alf, quickly taking it out of my hands.

"And this?" I enquired, pointing at a green tin with a big orange skull and crossbones on the back.

"Bubble bath."

Frank and Norman lived with Bob and Alf, an inseparable pair who had been together for many years in the long-stay hospital before being catapulted into their home in the community. Each morning they would go and collect their newspapers before waiting in their suits for the bus to the day centre. Frank had one eye, a club foot and was in constant pain, yet he was always laughing and at no time had I known him to laugh more than the day I had to cut Norman's toenails.

As well as management responsibilities for the home I was also required to help the men with their personal care. On one occasion, whilst bathing Norman, I noticed that his toenails were in a shocking state. Having recently completed toenail training (non-mandatory), I arranged to get a special clipper and cut them the next day.

When I arrived, the other residents were gathered in the front room to watch the event. With seven eyes on me I delicately peeled Norman's socks off to reveal the offending talons; they were long, curled and hornlike. A generous layer of cheesy substance had gathered underneath them and the smell made me dizzy. Urged on by the baying crowd I put the clipper around the first nail and squeezed.

Nothing.

I squeezed harder.

Still nothing.

Undeterred, I rolled my sleeves up and knelt at Norman's feet. Using both hands I pushed with all my might.

And pushed.

And pushed.

Suddenly, without warning, there was a loud crack and half an inch of rancid nail flew off Norman's toe and straight into my mouth. As it hit the back of my throat with a sharp tang, I lost balance and fell backwards, the sound of Frank's laughter ringing in my ears.

Years later a similar incident was to occur when I was working on the duty desk of a mental health team. An irate service user, eating a bag of crisps and shouting furiously at me about his housing situation, launched a piece of potato high into the air from his mouth. I winced as it landed on my tongue and the taste of cheese and onion filled my mouth. I winced again when I looked down and saw he was holding a bag of Ready Salted crisps.

SIX

Once I had dealt with the toxic bubble bath, photoshopped pornography and nine-year-old toenail cheese, things went well at the men's house and before long I was asked to manage other homes in the area. I accepted this challenge with gusto and soon found myself being drawn into the squalid world of low-level management, where you got excited about petty cash spreadsheets and eagerly anticipated the outcome of stationery audits. Luckily, I was still required to balance my management responsibilities with my support worker role and nothing kept me grounded more than Patricia castigating me for getting shampoo in her eyes or Wilfred, on asking him why the television he was watching snooker on had a tea towel draped over the screen, shouting that it was "so that the audience can't see me you bloody fool!"

Like the men's home, the other houses that I took on were also in a state of disrepair and I was keen to address this as soon as possible so that they did not stand out and draw unfavourable comment from the community. The properties were owned by a housing association that would happily take you to the Supreme Court if you were a day late on your rent but would take months to come out and fix a faulty water supply. When they finally did arrive, a fleet of vehicles would descend upon you, sending out the clear message that you were different from your home-owning neighbours.

After many futile weeks of pestering them to come out and replace a broken window I decided that I would take matters into my own hands and pay for a private handyman to do the work. Within a day, "Fix-it" Frank had sorted it out and so I promptly signed him up to a programme of work he could carry out on the other properties. The following week, as he was leaving one of the homes after repairing some guttering, we spoke about how positive the arrangement was for us both. He had a regular supply of work and I could access quick repairs from a discreet, local resource that did not mark the homes out as different. It was only as he drove off that I noticed the new sign on his van: Fix it Frank – specialist in the handicapped.

I knew that I would have to address why specialist in the handicapped did not really fit with our community ethos and so I phoned him late at night when I knew he wouldn't answer the phone so that I could leave a message.

He answered the phone.

After ten minutes of me bumbling about stigma and normalisation it was clear that Frank couldn't see my point. He just saw an unexploited market that he could make a lot of money from. In the end I gave up trying to explain and decided that I would use someone else.

I found an advert for Mr Gupta (You've tried the cowboys now call an Indian) and arranged for him to start working for us.

This was not to last long either.

"I've turned off all of the electric," he said to me one morning as I came into the kitchen to find him removing a plug socket, "I hope that's ok?"

"As long as it doesn't affect the people upstairs on life-support," I replied.

He threw down his screwdriver and ran for the fuse box before I was able to tell him that we didn't actually have people upstairs on life-support. When I did, he never saw the funny side and I never saw Mr Gupta again.

My days were a combination of planned visits and attending to crises and to help me with the latter, my manager gave me a state-of-the-art pager which was the size and weight of a toaster. Intensely proud of this miracle of technology, I strapped it to my belt (with the help of a colleague to lift it) and strutted around, desperate for the bloody thing to go off.

Only once did this happen, when I was in the middle of a shopping spree at my local Weigh-and-Save store. On hearing its beep, I dramatically threw down my scoop of frozen gooseberries and ran to a nearby phone box. With trembling hands I frantically dialled the number on the screen, imagining all manner of emergencies that I would need to avert. Time after time I tried; time after time I got a dead tone. It was only when the skin on my fingertip started to flay that I remembered I had turned the lottery update option on earlier in the week and had just spent the last twenty minutes phoning the week's winning lotto numbers (plus bonus ball).

Though my pager would remain silent for evermore, I still felt like a manager who was going places, a man in control, a mover and shaker in the high-flying world of supported living. There wasn't a problem I couldn't solve, a person I couldn't help.

Until I met Malcolm.

Malcolm was another man who had spent most of his life in a long-stay hospital before being forcibly resettled into his own flat and promptly forgotten about. Environmental health, social services and the police had all been called many times by neighbours who were concerned with some of the noises and smells coming from his home. Malcolm had consistently refused all offers of help and so my organisation had been given a contract to try and engage with him and avoid him being made homeless.

Information about Malcolm was scarce and so, as I drove to my first visit with him, the only things I knew were that he was 6'3" and weighed twenty-two stone.

And was highly volatile.

The welcome that Malcolm showed me on that initial meeting was to be repeated many times in the years to come.

"Hello Malcolm," I would say, warmly holding out a hand.

"What do you want, little man?" he would reply, ignoring my hand and purposely stepping on my toes with his size sixteen shoes.

We would then go into his flat where I would try to press upon him how close he was to being evicted whilst he pretended I wasn't there.

The main reason that eviction was imminent was due to the dire state of the flat. Since moving in many years ago, he had managed to hoard an impressive collection of wood off-cuts, biscuit tins and railway magazines, sourced from all over the county and brought home on his pushbike-trailer hybrid creation. Though he had cleaved a complex network of passages into the clutter, allowing him to navigate around his home, Malcolm had managed to ensure that every room was waist-deep in waste. A strong smell of petrol hung permanently in the air and flies circled madly in the kitchen. There were no pets allowed but a regular scuttling could be heard in the far corners of the room and an unnamed creature would occasionally brush past your foot. Most remarkably, a small model train set wove its way over the debris, diving off McVitie tins in the living room, veering over broken MDF panels in the hall and climbing issues of Railway Monthly up the stairs. As it chugged along, powered by a complex grid of exposed electrical cables, Malcolm would flit around it, hammering on impromptu sidings and ad hoc diversions to ensure that the little engine never stopped.

Over time I tried hard to forge a positive relationship with Malcolm, in the hope that I could have some influence on his housekeeping. When he complained of hearing loss I took him to the doctor who, on gingerly peering into his ears, nearly dropped his otoscope. A course of industrial strength ear drops later and the GP was syringing two thick slugs of brown wax into a metal kidney bowl I had been asked to hold.

"I can hear my footsteps!" exclaimed Malcolm as he happily tapped his feet and I fought hard not to vomit.

When he had toothache I promptly whisked him to the dentist for a root canal, promptly whisking him away when he threatened to rip the dentist's throat out if he caused him any discomfort.

And, when his size sixteen shoes finally wore through, I drove him to the oversized men's shop in the next county so that he could buy a new pair with which to crush my toes.

Yet despite all of my efforts, the flat remained in a filthy state. In desperation I rented a skip which was subsequently used by everyone in the close except Malcolm, who would then pick through it at night and take armfuls of junk back to his flat.

Eventually, after years of working with him, a breakthrough came. One fine day, as I read him the latest notice to quit letter from the housing association, Malcolm expressed an interest in getting a shed to store some of his wood. No sooner were the words out of his mouth then we were in the car and hurtling towards B&Q. As Malcolm had a large garden he barely used, we plumped for a spacious 8' x 6' shed. Malcolm was insistent that he built it himself whilst I wanted to pay for the professional assembly option. However, limited finances and a fear of scuppering the deal weakened my negotiating position and we eventually compromised that we would build it together.

Delivery was arranged for the weekend and I turned up early Monday morning with my power screwdriver and tool belt. As I approached the house the shed was nowhere to be seen. I rang the bell and Malcolm answered the door, grinning.

"Hello little man," he said, stepping on my toes.

I followed him into the front room where the shed stood, fully assembled and full of wood off-cuts, biscuit tins and railway magazines.

That afternoon I applied to go back to university.

SEVEN

A longside photographs of bohemian students playing Frisbee and exotic supermodels standing around a Bunsen burner, the prospectus for my local university outlined two routes for gaining a professional social work qualification: a Diploma or a Masters.

In order to be considered for the latter I would need to demonstrate that I possessed a relevant degree. I decided that I would go for this and several months later, in my entrance interview, I found myself being asked by a dour professor what I thought the relevance of my archaeology degree was to social work.

"An interest in older people?" I ventured.

To my great surprise and anxiety, I soon received a letter offering me a place on the next Masters in Social Work course. My voluntary work, current job, management experience and work with children had all come together to enable me to be chosen over many of the other applicants.

Or, as one of my colleagues surmised, "It's because you're a white male."

I nervously told my manager about my success (and the fact that I had used her as a reference without asking her permission) and was relieved that not only was she not going to take legal action against me, but she also suggested that I continued to work for her on a part-time basis. I agreed immediately. Whilst she could be fearsome,

I loved working with the staff and the residents at the homes and the wages would supplement the small bursary I would receive. The course was fulltime but there would be plenty of opportunity for me to work in the evenings and at weekends. Unlike my first time at university there would be no drunken parties, no drug-fuelled raves, no naked bannister-sliding. I was a mature student now and I would be like all the other mature students I had known; committed, focussed and clinically depressed.

Over the summer I bought all of the course essentials (text books, stationery and a cardigan) and nervously waited for the first day of term. When it finally arrived I walked into the sleek, modern department and presented my acceptance letter to the stylish receptionist.

"I'm sorry," she said, scanning it, "this is the Mathematics department. You want that building over there."

She pointed to what looked like a milking shed.

There were twelve other people in my class. All were female except myself and Jimmy Wanzala, a tall man from Swaziland who had four wives and a bad back. An empty seat at the front belonged to Titsy, a mysterious student who, despite never once making an appearance, would have her name called out on the daily register for the next two years. When lectures on radical social theory or the epidemiology of poverty became too much, I would find myself daydreaming about what Titsy was up to.

Negotiating a tense hostage situation?

Paragliding into a secure military compound?

Assassinating a head of state?

Working in Asda?

Our opening lecture was on anti-discriminatory practice and I was anxious not to offend anyone's race, gender, ethnicity, sexuality, religion, disability or age on my first day. After a brief introduction, we were put into pairs and asked to feedback our partner's background to the rest of the class. I was with Fiona, an agony aunt for a national newspaper, and so I was able to talk about her career before she followed with mine. At the end our tutor, a fearsome ex-social worker who had last practiced in the reign of George V, came to the front.

"Isn't it interesting," she said, beckoning the next pair up, "how the man always goes first."

I looked down, shamefaced at oppressing a gender in my first ten minutes.

Worse was soon to follow.

In a sociology lesson later that week, Helen, one of the older class members, commented on how men had a tendency to be aggressive.

"MEN ARE NOT AGGRESSIVE!" I screamed at her.

Unfortunately, Helen did not see this as the ironic riposte that I had intended and promptly reported me to our head of year. I was summoned to the staff room where I tried to explain that I wasn't a sexist with anger management issues. Luckily I was given the benefit of the doubt but would spend the next two years worrying about being thrown off the course.

Perhaps I shouldn't have.

In a subsequent lecture on transactional analysis (a theory of communication which identifies people's exchanges on either a child, adult or parent level) the tutor assured us that no one ever failed a social work course so there was really no need to worry (parent to child).

*

Through a perfect storm of university slackness and social work woolliness, the course trudged on with frequent cancellations, double-booked rooms and general confusion. In our law module, the usual tutor had left and so a replacement had to be found at short notice. It soon became clear that the new man knew nothing about social work law and sought to mask this by spending an entire term telling us about the composition of the House of Lords. I imagined in years to come what I would say when asked by a judge under what power I had removed the child.

"No idea, m'lord, but I know where Earl Baldwin of Bewdley sits."

There was one serious lecturer within the faculty (who probably wandered in thinking it was the Mathematics department and was never allowed to leave) and her discipline, hidden within the cloud of vagary that her colleagues excreted, took the whole class by surprise. Starting in the second term, we mooched into her lesson, unaware of the perils that lay ahead. The first sign that this lecture was going to be different was the digital clock that she carefully placed on her desk. The second sign was that, on the stroke of nine o'clock, she walked over to the door and locked it. Those of us who had managed (mostly by chance) to be in before this deadline watched over the course of the lesson as our classmates ambled up to the door and found that none shall pass.

They would knock but were ignored.

They would call but were ignored.

They would rattle the handle, kick the door, bang the glass and shout obscenities, but were ignored.

By the end of the lesson there were a group of miserable faces pressing against the steamed-up window, like poor Victorian street urchins peering into a sweetshop. On one occasion, a stranger's face looked longingly in before turning around sadly and leaving. It was only later that it occurred to me that this might have been Titsy.

The most enjoyable lesson of the year was sign language which had been hastily organised by Alison, a student in our class who was deaf. As well as teaching me to sign badminton and blow job (not to be mixed up at the local leisure centre), Alison and her best friend, Anika, would often invite me around to their room on campus to do coursework, watch episodes of Friends and play Luigi's Mansion on the Nintendo.

During this time, my wife and I had been going through a difficult patch. We had been together for ten years but changes in our values, different goals and meeting a breakdown recovery driver called Paul (her not me), resulted in us separating. This happened quickly and, one summer's evening, I agreed that I would move out of our flat. I did this without giving much thought to the fact that I had nowhere else to go and so, at nine the following morning, having spent the night in my car on the forecourt of a twenty four hour petrol station, I was queuing outside the university's student centre for somewhere to live.

The student advisor, perhaps sensing my desperation and perhaps smelling the diesel fumes emanating from me, explained that because it was still the summer holidays there was plenty of accommodation available and handed me the keys to a room in A Block. With a small bag of possessions, I trudged up the stairs looking for my room. I turned the corner and bumped into Alison and Anika. In my emotional turmoil it hadn't registered with me that they also lived in A Block.

"Come on in," they said, unaware of my major life event and thinking I had just popped round for a quick go on Luigi's Mansion. I followed them in and ended up staying for several hours, unable to disclose my difficult predicament.

"I best be off then," I said eventually, striding confidently out of their door before sneaking back down the corridor to find my new room.

The next morning I bumped into them in the kitchen.

"You're back?" said Alison, a note of surprise in her voice and a mild look of fear in her eyes.

As I could think of no other reason to explain why I was eating Coco Pops at 7 am in the communal kitchen, I had to disclose my major life event.

I managed another month in the halls of residence before I fled. Apart from Alison, Anika and I, the only other residents at the university were a large contingent of Chinese students. Unfortunately their body clocks appeared to still be on China time and, at 3 am every morning, they would all go to the kitchen (next to my room) and cook a large banquet. The walls were thin and, with no option of building a cooler box and pickled onion jar sound barrier, I would be left to lie awake, listening to their happy chatter.

After weeks of sleep deprivation I snapped and left the halls.

Where can I go, I wondered, that will be quiet, cheap and still retain my dignity?

For the rest of the course I lived in my ex-mother-in-law's spare room.

EIGHT

I was desperate to start planning for the future and stop dwelling on the past, and resolved that I would take on as many bank shifts as possible so that I could start to save up for my own flat. Whilst my mother and father-in-law were undoubtedly warm, caring people, there were only so many times you could reminisce about family gatherings you'd attended with their daughter when the daughter in question was currently in your marital bed making the beast with two backs with the fourth emergency service.

After going to meet with my service manager and explaining my delicate predicament to her, she naturally took full advantage of my desperation and asked me to focus on a number of tasks that lent themselves to evening work and which she had been having difficulties allocating.

I would be her gun for hire.

An agent in the field.

A special operative.

A depressed divorcee doing the jobs that other people would rather not do.

My first assignment was to carry out an internal audit of all the care homes in the area and I set to work arranging meetings with the various managers to inspect their premises. Whilst I wasn't expecting to be greeted with open arms, I was surprised by the levels of antagonism aimed towards me and found the whole project enormously challenging. People who had worked in the industry for most of their lives were not receptive to a young whippersnapper with a workbook waltzing in and passing judgement on their abilities. But it did provide me with lots of new experiences and taught me a valuable lesson which I would carry with me for the rest of my career; namely that if you ever experience uncertainty in your own abilities, take a moment to consider all the other oddballs, cranks and social outcasts who work in the caring professions and you won't feel quite so bad about yourself.

The first home manager I met with was Desmond, who had driven for over forty years but never gone over a roundabout. Next, there was Vikki, who wanted to be a social worker but felt that she hadn't had enough adversity in her life to warrant it. She told me that she hoped to experience some soon. Barbara was never far from her bottle of 40% proof aperitif that she swigged throughout the day to alleviate her irritable bowel whilst Colin was a shy and retiring man who I struck up a good relationship with until he saw that I'd rated his ability to manage petty cash as poor and then he went completely ape shit.

Eventually, after weeks of uncomfortable meetings, I was able to present the finished report to my service manager (who promptly shelved it as it didn't reflect well on her ability to manage services) before moving onto my next task: one-to-one social trips with the residents.

I began by taking Edith to her fortnightly blind club where I would spend hours playing braille bingo, my ears pricked up, my dobber poised to dob. After months of sitting through the monotone Master of Ceremonies' clickerty clicks and droopy drawers I finally got my first line and rushed excitedly to the prize table, only to discover that there was but one prize left: a dented tin of Italian plum tomatoes.

I alternated my blind club weeks with taking Jimmy to watch his beloved football team, but was surprised, on picking him up for our first match together, to find that he was wearing the training coat of their fierce rivals.

"I just preferred the colours," explained Jimmy as we took our seats and went on to be subjected to ninety minutes of verbal abuse by the supporters around us.

Simon loved films and so we agreed that I would take him to the cinema. Unfortunately Simon also had Tourette's syndrome and it became clear on the way there that it might be best for everyone concerned if I found a reasonably loud film. When we arrived I surveyed the board: The Crying Game, Chaplin, Howards End. It seemed that I had picked the quietest film week in cinema history. In the end we plumped for a re-screening of Grease and I sat down, confident that Summer Loving, Greased Lightning and You're the One That I Want would drown out any unwanted outbursts. Unfortunately, I had forgotten about Sandy, Hopelessly Devoted to You and Tears on my Pillow or, as it was on that fateful night, PISS! on my Pillow.

Although challenging, these jobs enabled me to save money towards a deposit so that when an advert went up in my local library for a block of newly-built keyworker flats, I was in a position to apply. The flats were a response to the high cost of rent in the area and the difficulties that keyworkers such as nurses, police and firefighters had affording them. I took down the number, contacted the managing agency and, one week later, I was offered a flat which I immediately snapped up.

With a bed liberated from my old house and a framed photo of my wedding day (given to me as a leaving present by my in-laws), I moved into my flat and began to introduce myself to my new neighbours. The people in the flat above were librarians and seemed very pleasant. On one side of me was a young man who was a librarian whilst on the other side there was Emily. She was a librarian. I popped down to the flat below and a policeman answered.

"I've just moved in above and thought I'd say hello," I said.

"Pleased to meet you," he replied, shaking my hand, "but this place is actually my partner's. She's currently at work at the library."

Though the town's buildings may burn, its shops looted and its citizens left untreated in the hospital, at least we would be able to access a well ordered reference section.

Since this was the first place I had owned on my own, I was able to set it up exactly as I had always dreamt. I had pictures of my favourite rappers on the walls, my record collection was out and every games console I owned was spread across the floor. I was able to do what I wanted, when I wanted and with whom I wanted.

My God, I was miserable.

As well as having to keep very quiet on account of my neighbours' constant shushing, I had no idea what I should do with myself. During the day I went to university but, on the many nights that I wasn't at work, I sat on the floor swigging aperitif for my newly-emerged irritable bowel, watching the CCTV channel on my television. I had accidentally stumbled upon the channel when I was trying to tune in my Nintendo Pippin and, realising that it was a live feed of the building's CCTV cameras, I quickly became obsessed, always on the lookout for Colin coming for retribution after my aspersions on his ability to manage petty cash.

Colin never came but Janine did. A fiery librarian from the sixth floor, she was passionate about art (mostly carved into her arms) and would often undertake spontaneous performance pieces, such as throwing all of my bread out of the window in the dead of night for no discernible reason. As I watched in anguish as my floured baps hit the pavement below, she moved in close to me.

"Art is pain," she said tenderly, "art is pain."

Whilst Janine's energy and impulsiveness was to provide a timely distraction at this difficult point in my life, she eventually came close to killing me when, after having had a shower, she wrote me a loving message across the steamed-up Biggie Smalls picture in my bathroom. Unfortunately it disappeared before I had a chance to read it (though the greasy imprint left by Janine's finger did not). Later that evening, as I lay alone in the bath looking at Biggie, I asked him, as I often did, for guidance in my life. To my horror, as the room slowly filled with steam, a message appeared across his gaudy Gucci sweatshirt.

I'll always be here for you David.

I scrambled out of the bath, slipped on my flannel and lay writhing in agony on the floor.

"Help!" I called out, trying to alert my neighbours, "Help!"

Eventually someone heard me. "Shhhh!"

NINE

Each year on the course we were required to undertake a three-month work placement. It was difficult for the university to identify enough employers willing to take all the students and we were encouraged to find our own.

I immediately knew where I wanted to go.

Several months earlier I had attended a course which started with the instruction:

Get into small groups and write down all the sexually explicit words you can think of.

Three of us had sat around a sheet of flip-chart paper sheepishly.

"Dick?" said Rose eventually.

"Twat," I ventured.

"You've got to have pussy, I suppose," said Sheila from Age Concern.

The aim of the course was to help support people with a learning disability around issues of sexuality and the opening exercise emphasised the need to be comfortable with sexually explicit language in order to support people effectively. It was an important lesson though all I can remember is Rose, with marker in hand, asking if "poonanny" had two n's or three.

The course was run by a small team of NHS therapists who provided support to vulnerable people around issues of sexuality. This could range from the long-term victim of abuse to a young chap knocking one out in the communal television lounge. After being told I could do my first-year placement with the team, I was asked to begin working with the latter.

Gavin, the team leader, gave me the background to the referral, went through some suggestions for interventions and pointed me in the direction of the resource cupboard. I opened it and a wave of sex paraphernalia washed over me: a tsunami of rubber penises, flavoured condoms and scented lubricants. Scooping armfuls up off the floor, I eventually managed to get them all back before looking through some of the many books in the cupboard. I plumped for an old manual which showed drawings of appropriate and inappropriate places to undertake sexual activities including, most importantly for my purposes, a young chap knocking one out in the communal television lounge.

Public masturbation is a highly complex issue which can stem from numerous, interrelated factors. Communication difficulties, anger, frustration, disinhibition and past traumatic events can all contribute and, with long-term specialist counselling, significant change can be achieved. Me and a picture of a man masturbating in front of One Man and his Dog was going to have minimal impact.

Filled with insecurities and doubts about my ability to perform this task, I arrived at the young man's house and knocked on the door.

I am a sexpert, I told myself as I waited for someone to answer.

You know nothing about sex, myself answered.

I am a sexpert, I repeated.

You thought there was a penis bone.

I am a sexpert, I insisted.

Your girlfriend once played on her Gameboy whilst you were having sex.

I...

The door opened.

Summoning up all my confidence and trying to push painful memories of Tetris to the back of my mind, I introduced myself to the member of staff who reverentially ushered me into a room where poor Alan sat.

Like me, he was clearly terrified.

If the situation hadn't been quite so awful I may have sought to break the ice by pulling out a pair of jump leads and a car battery. But this was not the time and so I shut the door and we chatted about Star Wars figures until the allotted time was up.

On the way out I showed him the picture in the manual.

"Best not to do that Alan," I said, before returning to base.

Having reported back to Gavin that I had cured Alan of his affliction, he then asked if I was willing to take over the running of a group for men who had demonstrated various degrees of sexually inappropriate behaviour in the past. I was proud to be given this responsibility and was determined to make this project even more of a success than my work with Alan.

My first step was to go to a session run by Rick, a colleague who had led the group for several years and who would be handing the baton (enthusiastically) onto me. Each session, Rick explained, began with members telling the others about anything they had on their mind. Unfortunately, it had soon become clear to Rick that the men tended not to listen to a single word anyone else said. To combat this, he had devised a cunning system in which he would randomly ask someone to recap what the other person had said.

It had limited impact.

"And so my mum died on Tuesday, I was made homeless on Wednesday and arrested on Thursday," said a very distressed Neil.

"I'm really sorry to hear that," said Rick before turning to another group member. "John, could you tell us what Neil just said?"

"What?" said John, looking up from his Good Housekeeping magazine.

To try and capture their attention and stimulate lively debate I decided that I would introduce a bit of pizzazz into the group.

As the men wandered into my first session I dramatically turned out the lights, pointed a torch at John and cranked up the Who Wants to be a Millionaire? theme.

"John, you have a 50/50, ask the audience and phone a friend. How is AIDs transmitted: handshakes, kissing, the postal service or unprotected sex?"

"What?" said John, bewildered.

"Phone a friend?" I continued. "Peter, I'm with John and he needs your help. He's stuck on a question and so the next voice you hear will be his."

"I'm going home," he said and stomped off into the night.

The following week I tried Give us a Clue and met with similar levels of hostility, with Peter walking out once more after being asked to mime gonorrhoea in under two minutes. I quickly made the decision to abandon my gameshow format and so Family Fortunes, Mr and Mrs and Blankety Bank (which I was going to use to discuss masturbation - Wankety Wank) never saw the light of day.

Instead, I tried a different approach.

I tolerated silences, listened to the men's problems, empathised with them and encouraged others to do the same. To my great surprise it started to work and over the next few weeks the group soon became a safe place where the men could be themselves (until I got the whole service banned from the facilities because I let John smoke a joint in the library).

But it was an important lesson for me. I didn't need to have an agenda or provide all the answers. I had to let things be, and through time and patience I could build positive relationships with people who often didn't have many positive relationships in their lives.

As the weeks went by, I became close to my colleagues in this small team and enjoyed my days in the office, drinking tea and listening to the secretary talk about the problems of maintaining a five-bedroomed house on her own (I was in a one bedroomed flat haunted by the spirit of Biggie Smalls and so maintaining a five-bedroomed house didn't sound too much of an ordeal). Yet I was aware that a dark shadow loomed over the team: a shadow that belonged to a small, Welsh, sociopathic locality manager called Bridget.

Bridget had overall responsibility for the service and would visit unannounced each month, leaving a trail of distress and offence in her wake. I had briefly met Bridget on the first day of my placement. She had come up to me and asked what car I drove. I told her and enquired why she wanted to know. She explained that several days ago, in a hospital car park, a man in a blue BMW had driven past and waved at her. She had no idea who he was but had spent the last three days combing the locality to try and find him.

I did think this slightly odd, but it was to pale into insignificance when compared to the time, years later, that the team I worked for was visited by the local Conservative MP.

"And what are the main problems facing young people today?" he had asked Bridget.

"Anal sex," she said, without further explanation.

Of all Bridget's nuances, the most memorable could be seen during meetings with her. As she sat, listening intently or nodding vigorously, she would gradually pick bits of skin off her face until a small mound lay in front of her. She would then proceed to gather it together and roll it into a ball before popping it into her mouth and sucking it like a Werthers Original. She reportedly did this at every meeting and, as locality manager, she was required to attend a lot of meetings.

It was surprising there was anything left of her.

At one such meeting, several months after my placement had finished, she told Gavin that his team was being shut down. Pressures on funding meant that services, like her face, were being reduced on a daily basis.

TEN

Having successfully completed my placement with the sexuality support team, the social work course resumed at pace. Whilst the first year had meandered along, touching upon research, brushing against theory and examining the seating arrangements of the eight hundred and fourteen members of the House of Lords in forensic detail, the second year tried desperately to cram in everything else. For social work, the slackest of the slack, the woolliest of the woolly, this was impossible as it begged, borrowed and stole its ideas from a vast array of other disciplines and so I ended up having a brief taste of everything but felt as though I understood nothing. This was frustrating, but to be expected on a course that had only been running for forty six years.

The one area that was covered in depth was child protection and it was clear that the majority of my classmates were keen to go into this field.

I couldn't think of anything worse. My poor assertiveness skills made it impossible not to buy a jumper that I had unfolded in a shop, let alone remove a baby from their parents. My experiences as a youth worker and with my poo-toting niece had scarred me for life and left me with the unshakeable view that I should avoid working with children at all costs. Yet the majority of our lessons focussed exclusively on this whilst all the other major aspects of social work were glossed over and so, when I was told that my all-important, career-defining, final, second year placement would be in mental health, I panicked.

Apart from seeing my Cub Scout leader being taken away from a jamboree in an ambulance because he was frothing at the mouth, I was worried that I had no experience of mental illness. I confided this to my sister days before my placement was due to start.

"But what about Mum's job?" she asked.

My mum had worked in a psychiatric hospital and regularly brought patients home with her. Today, such blurring of work/life boundaries would result in instant dismissal, as it did for one of my colleagues who, when his line manager had called at his home unannounced during a period of sick leave, was found to have two service users doing his washing up. But then it was more accepted and I would often be in my bedroom happily playing Jet Set Willy when Tim, who had paranoid schizophrenia and believed he was Ian Brown from the Stone Roses, would come and tell me about an omnipotent society that wanted to suck all the information out of my brain via my eyeball.

"Thank you very much," I would politely reply, eight years old and unsure of the proper etiquette for receiving such news.

The Community Mental Health Service in which I would spend my second and final placement was a large multi-disciplinary team made up of social workers, nurses, psychiatrists, psychologist and a lone occupational therapist who carried a mysterious black bag around with her like an assassin. Only once did I see it open and I was disappointed to find that it did not contain a .38 calibre, high velocity sniper rifle but an assortment of rubber vegetables. My practice tutor was Hilary, an experienced social worker who I arranged to meet with on my first day. She explained that tensions were high in the team as weeks earlier there had been a coup in which the nurses had risen up as one and ousted the social work manager. The fallout had been considerable and professional allegiances had been formed. The university, having been made aware of the situation, offered me an alternative placement as they felt it was unfair to expect a student to work in such a hostile environment.

"We've found a small team," the placement officer told me, "that is really friendly, ten minutes from where you live and keen for you to start. The manager is experienced, they will pay all your travel expenses and the clients are very nice."

"And who are the clients?" I inquired.

"Children."

"No thank you," I said without missing a beat.

I'll take my chances with the team that wants to slaughter their own.

Hilary had identified a small caseload of people for me to work with during my placement and had marked each of their homes on a map.

"I thought it would help give you a sense of where everyone is," she said, handing it to me.

I looked at the red dots which were in the shape of a pentagram and resembled a serial killer's hunting pattern rather than a guide to my new clients.

"Is that a mistake?" I asked, noticing one dot at the edge of the map, miles from the others.

"No, that's Sarah."

That afternoon we drove to see Sarah, who was an in-patient in a remote, out-of-area hospital. At this time, such placements were relatively rare but over the years they became much more common as NHS commissioners saved thousands of pounds closing local wards so that they could pay millions to use private companies' distant facilities.

In the car, Hilary described the circumstances of Sarah's admission to hospital. She had initially been assessed in A&E and, after agreeing that she needed to be in hospital urgently, a bed was sought. With no local beds available, an out-of-area placement was commissioned and an ambulance booked to take her there. Hilary, who had been present throughout the traumatic assessment, wanted to support Sarah in her admission to a facility that neither of them knew and agreed to follow behind in her car. Unfortunately, as they set out from A&E, the ambulance that Hilary was supposed to be following crossed the path of another ambulance and she ended up following the wrong vehicle for over two hours in the wrong direction.

Sarah arrived alone at the psychiatric hospital and Hilary eventually arrived at a clinic for dental reconstruction.

"Here we are," said Hilary as we finally arrived outside the vast hospital complex in which Sarah had been admitted, "follow me."

She shot off towards the reception whilst I scurried behind. Weaving through the entrance foyer, we dashed past the clinic rooms, around the restaurant and towards the back of the hospital where the décor became more worn, the lighting more drab. Negotiating a corridor filled with broken wheelchairs and trolleys full of linen, we eventually reached the locked, heavy door to the mental health unit.

Hilary knocked and a bewildered, grubby face appeared at the window.

Poor soul, I thought, before he opened the door and introduced himself as the ward manager.

He led us to a room at the end of a long ward.

"I'll leave you to it," he said before lumbering off.

Hilary went in first.

"Sarah?" she said gently, "Sarah?"

The room appeared empty, with clothes, books and food strewn across the floor.

There was no sign of Sarah.

As we turned to leave, a blood curdling cry went up from the corner. A woman ran towards us with bloodshot eyes and wild hair.

"Aaaa!" she shouted.

"Aaaa!" I shouted, nearly jumping into Hilary's arms.

What in God's name had I walked into?

Victorian asylums and possessed loons?

We were only five minutes away from Waitrose.

Still she came at us.

"Aaaa!" she continued.

"Aaaa!" I continued.

As she came within striking distance I hid behind Hilary, covered my eyes and waited for the end to come.

"Aaaa…ve you brought those crisps I asked for?"

"I have," said Hilary, producing a bag of Quavers, "and I got you some Jaffa Cakes."

"Lovely," said Sarah.

ELEVEN

Having met with Sarah, the most remote of all my red dots, I gradually started to meet with all of the other people on the list that Hilary had given me. Some were keen to meet, some more reluctant. Some were uncomfortable with a student being involved in their lives, others were more welcoming.

"At last," said Max (one of the latter) after I had introduced myself, "a P.A."

Max, a previous high-flyer in the city, had become depressed following the loss of his marriage, his children, his home and his ten years of abstinence from Class A drugs. He had come to the attention of mental health services when his ex-wife, on returning home with a group of friends one evening, had found Max with his head in an electric oven filled with rhubarb leaves. Struggling to think straight, Max had obviously amalgamated several suicide methods resulting not in instant death, but a nasty cough, a green hue to his nose and a visit from the psychiatric liaison nurse.

Max was staying in a local homeless shelter and so we began by completing an application for the housing register. After amassing all the accompanying letters of support and evidence I dropped the application in at the council and waited for a response. Meanwhile Max, who still had contact with his old friends from the city, had been invited on a week away with them. Because Max was homeless the council had ten days to respond to our application. After hearing nothing for two weeks I phoned them with all the anger and indignation of an unqualified student.

"This man," I puffed at the housing officer, "has got nowhere to go and his mental health is deteriorating rapidly. Why haven't you fulfilled your statutory obligations?"

"Well," replied the officer, leafing through a file, "my notes say that we contacted him two days after the application was submitted but he told us that he couldn't talk as he was on a ski lift in Biarritz."

Max was eventually housed and, in a dramatic departure from his former life, became an eco-survivalist, shunning all of modern society's trappings (apart from the weekly payment from the benefits agency) to live off the land. I would often see him foraging for food in the most unlikely places: picking blackberries next to the motorway, elderflowers from the library gardens, nasturtiums from (slightly disgruntled) people's hanging baskets.

The last time I saw him he was in the middle of a roundabout with a large Tupperware and a handful of leaves.

I gave him a toot and prayed they weren't rhubarb.

Along with housing advice, supporting people with their finances was central to the social worker role. The fact that I was badly overdrawn on my current account and behind on three credit card repayments did not deter me from pontificating on the importance of sound financial management. Like housing, bereavement, relationships, assertiveness, healthy living, food hygiene, stress management and toenail care, I knew the theory but struggled to apply it to my own life.

Sonia was referred to our team after she had become distressed in the Citizens Advice Bureau whilst trying to deal with her debts. Their advisor was concerned about some of the things that Sonia had said and sent an urgent request for us to see her. They hadn't specified exactly what these concerns were and so I went to see her at her home to find out more.

Sonia welcomed me in and, after explaining who I was and why I was there, we sat for a while watching a daytime cookery programme together.

"So," I said eventually, pulling myself away from an item on giblets three ways, "I understand that there's a problem with money?"

"Well," she began and, without taking her eyes off the screen, she proceeded to explain that last year her boyfriend had flown her to Addis Ababa where she had stayed with a thalidomide dwarf who had convinced her to invest in his dubious luggage business. She had promptly returned to England and illegally re-mortgaged her ex-husband's house by forging his signature. Her ex-husband, who had previously kept her locked in the kitchen whilst he went to work, had reported this all to the police, her boyfriend had disappeared and she was due to go to court next month. She was being threatened with eviction and her much loved son had disowned her.

"But there's worse…" she continued.

My pencil snapped.

Worse?

Worse than an evil thalidomide dwarf from Addis Ababa?

"It's the people with the hollow eyes and keys on their tongues. They've found out where I live. They keep appearing on the walls and so I have to paint over them. At my last house they kept coming back and so I knocked down the kitchen wall with a sledgehammer."

As I got to know Sonia better it became clear that the former (arrest for embezzlement) was true and the latter (faces with keys for tongues) was not, and due to a psychotic illness. The day after our initial meeting I took Sonia to see the team's new psychiatrist who prescribed an antipsychotic that would reduce her hallucinations and delusions. Sonia would continue to see this psychiatrist whilst I would eventually marry her and we would have three children together (the psychiatrist, not Sonia). And, after meeting with solicitors, police, housing officers and bank managers, the various threats and charges against Sonia were dropped and she was able to rebuild her life and relationship with her son.

Throughout the course we were continually being told about unconditional positive regard, a concept developed by Carl Rogers in which there is a fundamental acceptance and support of a person regardless of what they said or did.

Carl had clearly never met Nigel.

Nigel's passions were takeaway food and pornography and when I first met him he was indulging in both.

"What you gonna do about this fucking flat?" he said,

swallowing a piece of tandoori chicken and turning the volume down on the Witches of Eastdick.

The flat in question was covered in dog faeces and dried skin. Nigel was locked in a nasty and long-running battle with the council for a move to another property. He thought he should be in a house with a garden. The council didn't agree. In protest he had set out on a campaign to make his flat uninhabitable or, in the words of the National Assistance Act criteria he sought to meet, a verminous condition. As a result, Nigel's flat, beard and underpants were now in a terrible state of neglect.

As I introduced myself and explained the powers that I had to help with his move (none), Nigel's beloved jet-black Doberman Pinscher sniffed hungrily at my testicles. This dog, and Nigel's love for it, was soon to be the focus of a psychotherapy discussion group I presented Nigel's case at.

"Clearly this animal represents Nigel's psyche," announced the psychotherapist after carefully listening to my overview of the situation. "He sees it as an extension of himself, a reflection of his potential and embodiment of his aspirations. What's the dog's name?"

"Shadow," I told her.

"Exactly!" she clapped, jumping up from her seat in excitement.

Over time, with lots of persistence, enthusiasm and antiseptic hand wipes, I did help Nigel get himself and his flat back on track. I arranged for him to stay in respite care for a week whilst his flat was deep cleaned. During this time Shadow stayed with Danny, a charismatic support worker who was always willing to do the jobs that no one else wanted to do.

One morning I saw Danny being dragged across the park by Shadow, who was trying to eat a squirrel.

"You bastard!" he shouted at me as he shot past.

As I watched him disappear into the sunset Danny's voice drifted back to me on the wind. "And he's shat all over my front room!"

As Nigel and I got to know each other he would tell me fantastical tales of his old life: of wild adventures in the army, a European love child, romances with glamorous heiresses. I listened patiently but sceptically, sure in the knowledge that he had not travelled far beyond the Indian restaurant on the high street.

Unfortunately, years of hard drinking were eventually to take their toll on Nigel's liver and, one summer's day, as we were nearing the end of our work together, he suddenly passed away. This was a big shock to me but I took solace in the fact that when he died he had a clean flat, clean beard and (reasonably) clean underpants.

Some time later I was milling around the team office when the secretary called up. There was a girl in reception that she was struggling to understand as she only spoke a little English. Could I speak any German, she wondered? I went down to see her, hoping she wanted to know the way to the castle or to order two sausages and a slice of cake. She didn't and after several minutes of trying to find out what she wanted I gave up. Luckily, a nurse in the team spoke German fluently and she was due back any minute. I took the girl upstairs and waited for Gabi to arrive.

After a while Gabi joined us and the two of them embarked on a long conversation whilst I nodded sagely, understanding nothing. Eventually Gabi turned to me and explained that she was trying to track down her father. She had received a letter from her dad, many years ago, that said he was living in the area and, knowing that he had struggled with alcohol, the girl had been advised to start her search at the mental health team. She reached into her pocket and passed me a photo.

It was of a young, happy Nigel in an army uniform with his arm around a glamorous heiress.

I explained, via Gabi, that I had got to know her dad over the last few months but unfortunately…

"Can I meet him?" she asked eagerly.

…but unfortunately he had died several weeks ago.

The girl wept.

I got her a phone and she spoke with her mum in Germany.

"Where is he buried?" she asked, after finishing the call.

I wasn't sure but after some enquiries I found the crematorium her dad had been taken to. I offered to drive her to it and the three of us went straight away. We arrived and explained the situation to the receptionist. She disappeared for a while and then appeared with an urn.

"As there was no one available to dispose of these we kept them in storage. Would you like to scatter them in our gardens?" she asked.

The girl looked at Gabi and I. We nodded.

I returned to my car and watched her scatter her dad's ashes in the distance.

After all these years she had finally found her father, and Nigel had finally got his garden.

TWELVE

The social work course dribbled to an end, much as it had started. Lectures ground to a halt, assignments petered out and, at a lavish ceremony in the milking shed, we were presented with our certificates and, ominously, a freephone number for a local counselling service.

Though the course had been a slog, I had enjoyed my placement with the Community Mental Health Team and was excited when the service manager asked me whether I would be interested in applying for a recently vacated post with the team. I was and I did and, after attending an interview, I successfully gained my first paid social worker job. Within hours of starting I was given advice on the importance of stress management and not burning myself out before being given a bulging caseload and told that I would be working on the duty desk the next day.

The duty desk was the heart of the service, a place where anyone could, and did, call. Whilst I would eventually come to enjoy the variety and unpredictability of the work, initially it filled me with dread. I would sit and stare at the phone, willing it not to ring. There was no specific training for duty and workers brought a range of approaches to the role. Maggie, a long-serving social worker counting the days to her retirement, would invariably steer any call onto the subject of literature. A man contemplating whether or not to jump off a railway bridge would, after half an hour with Maggie, climb down and go and borrow a copy of The God of Small Things from their local library. Jenny, a gung-ho Community Psychiatric Nurse and leading light in the National Trust would, more often than not, sign up the poor sods who phoned for help to a month's hard labour at a conservation project in the Orkney Isles she was involved with. And Gary (profession unknown) would repeatedly tell people I hear you, I hear you, whilst absentmindedly scratching his scrotum.

It all felt a bit haphazard.

The duty desk was always manned by two people: an experienced worker and a more junior member of staff. Of all the experienced workers, Jim was the king of duty. He had done it for years and had faced every possible scenario several times. Undaunted by anything that was thrown at him, he would deal with call after call whilst I cowered behind the desk. There were two phones in the duty room and I had perfected the technique of picking up the receiver milliseconds after Jim had already answered.

Together with his skills on duty, Jim was known for his temper which could be unleashed on anybody, at any time.

One morning I arrived in the office to find him screaming obscenities at his computer. "This fucking mouse has broken again!" he shouted, banging it furiously on the desk, "Why we can't go back to paper fucking files I'll never know!"

It was only when he had calmed down that he noticed it was not his mouse that he had been holding but a tin of Fisherman's Friends.

Although duty work was often frenetic, there could be days when the phone never rang. On one of these days I suggested that we play the traditional, and much loved, parlour game of who could say the word cunt the loudest.

"You're on," said Jim enthusiastically.

I was to start.

"Cunt," I whispered, looking around to see if any of my colleagues had heard.

"Cunt," followed Jim more confidently.

The game continued for some time, the volume escalating with each turn.

"CUNT!" shouted Jim after many more rounds.

Maggie popped her head round the door. "Did you call me, Jim?"

On another quiet day in duty, our colleague Samuel came in for a chat. As he sat on the desk the phone began to ring.

"Pick up that phone and answer it in a funny voice," I dared.

Without pause for thought he picked it up.

"Hello?" he squeaked.

Samuel's eyes widened in horror; the type of horror that comes from answering the phone in a shrill squeak to Dr Gilbert, the intimidating lead GP.

Dr Gilbert, the intimidating lead GP who was head of commissioning mental health services.

Dr Gilbert, the intimidating lead GP who was head of commissioning mental health services and who wanted to urgently refer a young woman with post-natal depression.

Samuel had to make a quick decision. He could either revert to his usual deep tone, thus acknowledging that he had put on a comedy voice to answer the duty phone, or continue in the same pitch.

He chose the latter.

As Jim and I looked on in amazement, Samuel took the whole referral in falsetto.

Each duty day had a one-hour morning and afternoon assessment slot which would be used to see people with a variety of difficulties. Low mood, high mood, no mood, hearing things, seeing things, seeing no one, withdrawn, overdrawn, overworked, unemployed, struggling with children, struggling without children, alcohol, illicit drugs, legal highs, legal troubles, obsessive compulsive disorder, personality disorder, anxiety disorder, overeating, undereating, distressed, disinhibited, living for tomorrow, wanting to die today.

The slots were always fully booked.

The two duty workers would take an assessment each and, if the thought of answering the phone to someone in distress filled me with anxiety, meeting them face to face took things to a new level of terror. In those first months I felt a huge expectation to solve a person's problems in the allotted hour. Yet I was usually unable to understand the problem within this time, never mind come up with a solution. But eventually, like the men's group, I came to realise that by being attentive and empathetic I could usually make some difference. I would occasionally offer practical advice but, for the most part, I just listened.

*

As well as duty assessments in the office we would also go and see people in the community if needed.

One morning we received a call from a concerned GP who had just returned from a home visit. His patient, Fatima, had struggled with obsessive compulsive disorder for many years but he felt that things had deteriorated dramatically in the last few months. Her obsessions were preventing her from leaving home and she was now struggling to look after herself. We agreed that we would see her immediately and so a doctor and I went to her house that afternoon.

We arrived at the address and knocked tentatively on the back door. There was no reply and so we knocked louder and louder. After five minutes it was clear that Fatima wasn't in, or if she was, she wasn't going to answer. I looked around the side of the house for another way in. There was a window slightly ajar. I opened it and peered in.

"Sweet baby Jesus!" I exclaimed, beckoning my colleague to come and look.

"Dolce bambino Gesu!" she exclaimed (she was Italian).

Inside were hundreds and hundreds of boxes, perfectly stacked on top of each other, floor to ceiling.

We stood together, taking in the scene. This was obsessive compulsion on a scale that neither of us had seen before. It was deeply unsettling.

We stood in silence.

"Hello?"

A voice from behind startled us both. We turned to find a little man looking up at us.

"Can I help you?" he asked.

"We're looking for Fatima?" I said, showing him my I.D. badge.

"Well she won't be in there," he replied, "that's my toy shop. She lives in the flat above."

THIRTEEN

I started working with Amanda in June and in August she killed herself. My manager called me into her office, told me the news and suggested I take some time off.

"For how long?" I asked, wondering if I could manage a trip abroad to distract me.

"Twenty minutes?" she suggested.

As well as the personal grief that came from the death of a 19-year-old woman who I was slowly getting to know, the impact on my ability to work was huge. Suddenly, all the people I saw who felt overwhelmed or under the weather sent me into a panic. Whereas I would previously have talked issues through in a calm and measured way, I now became paralysed with fear. I shifted from focussing upon people to focussing upon risk management, ensuring every form was up-to-date, every decision discussed with every team member.

It was exhausting.

I felt a sense of responsibility that was all-consuming. I constantly questioned what I could have done differently.

Would Amanda still be alive if I'd done more home visits?

Should I have pushed her more to disclose what she was thinking?

In time I came to realise that we have only a small influence on people's lives; when someone gets a promotion, moves into their own flat, feels better, it is to their credit, not ours.

But when they kill themselves we feel entirely responsible.

Sometime after her death, Amanda's parents invited me over to their house to talk. I was anxious about this because I was limited in what I could discuss and I didn't want to make them feel any worse than they already did. As I nervously walked up the drive, Amanda appeared at the door.

I stopped in shock.

"You're here to see my mum and dad?"

I nodded.

"I'll just go and get them."

Her parents invited me in and we talked over tea; they talked, I sat in stunned silence. Eventually, it became clear that there were lots of things that I didn't know about Amanda.

She had been a singer in a band.

She had won medals in national horse riding trials.

She had an identical twin sister.

Fortunately, the demands of a bulging caseload meant that I was unable to isolate myself from risk for too long and I was soon back meeting all sorts of people in all sorts of situations.

Amy had been a member of a chanting sect which ostracised her when she rebuffed the group leader's seedy advances.

"Their members are everywhere," she would insist as I tried to reassure her that such paranoia was unfounded.

Eventually she decided that she wanted a fresh start in another area and so I presented her case to the housing panel. After I had told them about Amy's misguided beliefs about the pervasiveness of this sinister cult, two of the panel put their hands up to make a declaration of interest.

They were members.

Douglas suffered from paranoid schizophrenia and thought his ejaculations were controlled by the state. He would test this hypothesis many times a day and bring me charts with the results. Douglas was the gentlest, kindest man you could meet but he would regularly approach police officers and tell them that he thought he was going to kill someone. As a result, I would be hauled in front of a multi-agency protection panel where I would tell the assembled police, civil servants and probation officers that the only risk posed by Douglas was a repetitive strain injury to himself.

Indigo Sugar Star (changed by deed poll from Keith) was a burly man with long ginger hair and a plaited beard who would walk around town in a pink leotard and wellies, chewing on a stick. His house was full of Care Bears and his dream was to start a dance studio for animals. One day he answered the door to me in a white mink coat and fluorescent lycra bodysuit. During our meeting I gently inquired when he had started to dress so ... individually.

"On my 17th birthday," he recalled angrily, "my mum bought me a navy-blue sweatshirt and I just thought enough is enough."

One day Indigo asked me if I could help him to move

to some new accommodation in a distant city that he had always wanted to live in. Always keen to help people to realise their dreams (and get them out of my catchment area), I agreed and, arriving there late one evening, he directed me to pull over by a field.

"Here we are," he said getting out of my car and pointing at a very large oak tree, "home."

I watched in disbelief as he proceeded to climb onto its main bough, unfurl his yoga mat and start placing Funshine Bear, Good Luck Bear and For the Love of God Could Someone Please Notify the Police Bear amongst its branches.

Lucy also loved teddy bears and was never without her favourite one, which she would dress according to the activity being undertaken. If we went for lunch it would be wearing a dinner jacket; at the cooking group, a chef's hat and apron; on holiday, a small pair of Speedos, sunglasses and a faint whiff of suntan lotion.

One day I was called by Ambulance Control to say that Lucy was behaving erratically in the town hall. I went down there and was told by the paramedics on the scene that they had tried to talk to her but were unsure what was wrong.

I said I'd take a look.

Minutes later I emerged. "She's hypomanic," I said with authority.

"How do you know?" they asked, clearly impressed with my diagnostic skills.

I produced her teddy bear from behind my back.

It was dressed as Buzz Lightyear.

*

Ray was an elderly man who had suffered from bipolar disorder all of his life. In his youth he had been a prolific criminal, robbing jewellers, estate agents and banks throughout the country. He would tell me about his biggest jobs and how he had managed to abscond from all manner of police cells, prisons and secure hospitals. As he became less mobile I took him to see a huge, new nursing home that I felt may be suitable for him. We negotiated the surveillance cameras, security doors and I.D. checks and peered down the long entrance corridor. At the far end was a gaunt elderly man in a wheelchair who slowly started to move towards us.

After several minutes he arrived.

"They keep the dead alive here," he announced.

I turned to reassure Ray but he had already escaped.

Alice had been admitted to a women's hospital following a manic episode in which she had thrown paint over a lollipop lady and sang hits from the shows in the local mosque.

One evening I went to visit her on the ward after I had finished a long day on duty. When I arrived, it was eerily quiet and a storm raged outside.

"Where is everyone?" I asked the nurse in charge.

"In the lounge having a makeover with Alice."

Since the last time I had seen Alice she was being hauled into an ambulance singing Somewhere Over the Rainbow, I was slightly concerned by this and so I walked warily towards the room.

I pushed open the door and was confronted by a group of shadowy figures who, as one, started to move towards me.

I backed against a wall.

Suddenly, a flash of lightning lit up the room to reveal a set of blood-red, lipstick smiles that Alice had liberally daubed across their depressed faces.

I froze.

Somewhere in the background someone started to sing Chim Chim Cher-ee.

Though she was only twenty, Belinda hadn't left her mum's flat in five years. Shortly before she had last gone out, her dad had deserted them, she had dropped out of school and her mum had been diagnosed with fibromyalgia. We met when I did a home visit and we resolved to turn things around. We set a goal (to go to the local supermarket) and began to take small steps towards it. Each week we would walk further into town, me making inane small talk and Belinda hyperventilating whilst clinging tightly to a small animal ornament she carried with her. (I encouraged this as I had previously seen the power that such transitional objects held – when my son was struggling to go to primary school I used to give him my cigarette lighter to carry with him).

Eventually the day of the supermarket arrived and we nervously walked inside. We had discussed what was the worst thing that could happen – Belinda had speculated on her fears of fainting, being recognised by an old school friend or getting lost.

She had not considered a bomb scare.

We were in the fruit and veg aisle when an army van screeched to a halt outside and soldiers started flooding in.

"I need everyone to keep calm," bellowed a man in body armour.

I heard the ceramic ferret shatter in Belinda's hand.

Katie had cats.

Hundreds of them.

When we met, she was in hospital and keen to return home.

"All I want in life," she would tell me, "is a roof over my head and grazing land for my pussies."

Before she could go home, however, we had to make sure that her flat was habitable and so the ward liaised with Environmental Health to arrange a deep clean. Unfortunately, no one was aware of Katie's funerary arrangements for those (many) cats that had perished under her care.

In an attempt to cryogenically preserve them so that one day in the distant future they might be returned to her loving embrace, she crammed them into her freezer.

A freezer that she had turned off on the day of her admission to hospital.

Twelve weeks earlier.

At the start of a very hot summer.

Months later, I met the council worker who had had to clean Katie's flat and he told me that he still suffered regular flashbacks of the sight and smell that greeted him when he had opened the freezer expecting to find out-of-date fish fingers.

One morning I arrived at work to hear a heated debate

taking place in the large meeting room. I squinted through the frosted glass and could just make out a number of figures jumping around inside.

Mildly puzzled, I ambled down the corridor to the manager's office. "Is there a drama session going on, Hilary?"

Why I should have asked this, I am still unsure. There never was and, to the best of my knowledge, never had been a drama session in the large meeting room.

Or in any room.

I don't even know what a drama session is.

Before Hilary had a chance to tell me not to ask such bloody stupid questions a chair came flying through the large meeting room window. This was swiftly followed by the door bursting open and several of my colleagues rushing out.

A man strode out behind them.

"WHO WANTS IT?" he screamed, "WHO FUCKING WANTS IT?"

I certainly didn't want it.

Nor did Dr Singh, who sprinted into a side office and slammed the door, leaving Maggie (near retirement) abandoned in the corridor.

"WHO FUCKING WANTS IT?"

All around me colleagues dived under desks, hid behind filing cabinets and barricaded themselves behind doors.

Though we hadn't discussed it formally, it was clear that no one wanted it.

"WHO FUCKING WANTS IT??"

I ran into the photocopying room, suddenly realising that I had chosen the only room in the building that didn't have a door. I went to the far end and the man came in behind me and stood at the doorway.

"WHO FUCKING WANTS IT?"

Much has been written about two of the fear responses: fight or flight. There has been less said about the third one: photocopy.

Under his menacing stare I proceeded to print off ream upon ream of blank A3. Eventually he turned and left.

"WHO FUCKING WANTS IT?"

Finally, as workers offered up prayers, phoned loved ones, and tried furiously to scribble their last will and testimony onto post-it notes, our eighteen-year-old admin assistant walked up to the man.

"Do you want to leave?" she asked.

"WHO FUCKING W…yes please."

She pointed to the exit and he left.

FOURTEEN

Many of the service users I worked with during this time had, at some point in their lives, required compulsory admission to hospital under the Mental Health Act. The Act allowed people with a mental health problem, who posed a risk to their own health or safety or the safety of others, to be detained against their will. This process of sectioning was led by an Approved Social Worker and, as a qualified practitioner in mental health, I was expected to complete the course. With encouragement from my colleagues, who felt it would develop my practice (and allow them to do less days on the rota), I signed up for the three-month programme. The course was highly regarded but I felt anxious that, after a few lectures, exams and essays, I would be able to deprive people of their liberty. My pottery night classes had required more of a time commitment and all I could do at the end of them was make a wonky sugar bowl.

In preparation for the course I was required to shadow a Mental Health Act assessment, attend a day at court and take part in a Mental Health Act Tribunal, though in hindsight, being patronised by a disgruntled policeman, having to wait for seven hours in A&E and trying to complete a statutory document correctly whilst being assaulted by a ninety-six-year-old would have been more appropriate preparation for what was to come.

The purpose of the Mental Health Act Tribunal was to review the grounds for people's detention and ensure that the legal criteria were met. The tribunal panel was composed of a barrister, psychiatrist and lay-person who would interview relevant members of staff and review the reports that the care team were required to submit. The detained person was also encouraged to attend with legal representation.

Although these panels were usually stressful for all concerned, they provided a valuable safeguard to vulnerable people and fulfilled Article Five of the Human Rights Act which required that anyone deprived of their liberty had speedy access to a court to review its lawfulness (knowledge of which would have been invaluable to me years earlier when, aged seven, I was imprisoned in the boot of a car by Danny "Deadleg" Niblett and his Sticky Knicky Crew).

With admissions under the Mental Health Act rising each year, tribunals took place regularly and soon after registering for the course I was given the name of a man who was due to have his case reviewed in the coming week. Colleagues had advised me that the more I put into the report the less questions I would be asked and so, fearful of becoming tongue-tied and unable to provide the relevant information leading to the panel upholding the appeal and the person's subsequent discharge, deterioration and slow, lingering death in the community, I set about writing The Complete Life and Times of Donald S (unabridged).

Donald S. was an elderly man who had served as a radar operator during World War Two. In one of several bulging case files I read how he would spend weeks lying in complete silence in the holds of merchant ships listening for enemy submarines. In later life he had been diagnosed with dementia and had needed increased levels of support in his home. After a series of falls, fires and fights it was reluctantly decided by his family that things couldn't carry on safely and he was detained in hospital. Donald hated it and promptly escaped by balancing a chair on a table and climbing out of a Velux window. He was desperate to return home but instead found himself being transferred to a more secure unit.

The tribunal was scheduled to see whether he should stay there.

I met with Donald on three occasions and during these hour-long sessions he didn't say a single word.

I saw him prior to the tribunal beginning and he didn't say a single word.

As the tribunal started and the barrister outlined the process we would follow, he didn't say a single word. As I strained to lift my report out of my bag and onto the table, he didn't say a single word. When I was cross-examined about his ability to return home, he didn't say a single word. When I was asked the only question I wasn't 100% certain of: whether the bathroom was upstairs or downstairs, he didn't say a single word. When I ventured that the bathroom was upstairs Donald immediately stood up and said, in a loud, clear voice, "This man is a damn liar. My bathroom is on the ground floor!"

The panel regarded me with disgust.

With cuts in hospital beds and community services, there was a constant stream of requests for a Mental Health Act assessment and so, within minutes of expressing a wish to shadow one, I was preparing to go out. Kirsty, the Approved Social Worker on duty, went through the forms with me.

"Now, you need to bring these to every assessment," she said, flicking through a bundle of pink papers, "and always take a phone and a banana."

Kirsty and I drove to the address to find two concerned parents waiting outside for us. Over the last few months their son had become increasingly withdrawn and isolated, fearing that someone, or something, was trying to harm him. He had stopped eating and drinking and was refusing any contact with health professionals. His GP, after many failed attempts to engage with him, had finally requested a Mental Health Act assessment. Unfortunately, for someone who is paranoid that they will be forcibly removed from their home, taken away in a van and locked up against their will, the response of social services is often to forcibly remove them from their home, take them away in a van and lock them up against their will.

Once this was explained to him, naturally he fled.

The police were called (phone) and I waited for over three hours (banana) with Kirsty and the two doctors.

"He's just got no self-esteem," said his parents, surrounded by framed photographs of their daughters being presented with degrees, diplomas, doctorates and Nobel Peace Prizes.

Eventually he was found and brought back to the home by four police officers. It did not take the assessing team long to decide that he needed to be in hospital.

"Pass me the forms," said Kirsty, reaching for her pen.

"The forms?" I asked.

When Kirsty had said that I needed to take the pink forms to every assessment I hadn't realised she had included this one. I rummaged through my bag, knowing full well they weren't there.

"Try the front pocket," suggested the distressed young man we were about to detain.

I did but it was empty. In the end I had to drive to the office, vowing on the way back that I would never forget them again.

I've done it about twenty times since.

As much Mental Health Act work required a sound knowledge of the legal system, we were also encouraged to attend a trial to familiarise ourselves with the courtroom setting. This would be particularly useful for when we needed to obtain a warrant to gain access to a person's home. I duly arrived at my local Crown court and chose a trial to attend – a case of aggravated assault following a neighbourhood dispute. As I sat alone in the empty public gallery I heard how the accused, a meek unassuming gentleman, was alleged to have attacked the victim with a broom in a row over chimney fumes. I was gripped by the arguments and counter-arguments and was even more intrigued when the defendant's barrister approached the judge, whispered a few words and the judge ordered the jury to leave. With the court cleared the judge announced to the prosecution that the defendant felt he was being intimidated from the public gallery.

They all turned and looked at me.

I gave my best social worker look (somewhere between compassionate and constipated), the judge overruled the point, the jury were ushered back in and the case against the poor man continued.

I'm glad to say that the paranoid bastard was eventually found guilty.

I would encounter the same judge many years later when I was required to give evidence on behalf of someone I worked with. As I was about to leave the office to attend the hearing I realised that I did not have my ID card with me; something which could lead to all sorts of difficulties.

"I'll write a letter to say who you are and explain what's happened," offered the always helpful (but slightly dyslexic) Hilary.

Thanking her profusely, I accepted her offer, waited whilst she wrote it and promptly rushed off to court.

"Have you actually read this?" asked the judge, as he got to the end of the letter.

I hadn't and so he passed it to a court clerk who brought it over to me.

It said that I had forgotten to bring my IQ into work with me today.

FIFTEEN

Having shadowed a Mental Health Act assessment, observed a criminal trial and taken part in a review tribunal, I was now ready for the Approved Social Worker training to start. The course was based at the university's city centre campus which meant that I would have to start commuting into lectures each day. I had always been envious of my friends whose jobs required a morning trip into the city and was excited that I would soon have the opportunity to get up at an ungodly hour, stuff myself onto an overcrowded carriage and be coughed over by diseased strangers.

The Approved Social Worker training course had been lovingly developed and delivered by Mavis for the last twenty years. Mavis knew everything about the Mental Health Act, had been involved in its drafting and could draw upon her vast experience of sectioning people; from the person she assessed the previous night, whilst working for the emergency duty team, right back to Rasputin. Mavis taught most of the lessons and as well as her wealth of knowledge, brought with her a constant cough which she insisted on treating exclusively with Tudor-age herbal remedies. As she wheezed and spluttered through lecture after lecture the class would will her to swallow a handful of Neurofen rather than continue dabbing at her nettle and diggleweed poultice.

When the first day of the course arrived, I was determined to immerse myself into the metropolitan urbanite hipster lifestyle. I drank overpriced coffee, bought salads that tasted of hedge and started wearing flamboyant knitwear. Lectures were scheduled to start at ten and so, after a brief visit to an exhibition on pre-industrial Nepalese paperweights, I found the university hall and sauntered in, knowing from previous courses that the first day was always a relaxed, low-key affair, filled with ice-breakers, introductions and overviews. Casually taking my seat, I took off my beret and finished my bracken tabbouleh.

"Right," announced Mavis, coming to the front of the room with a group of vaguely familiar-looking people, "today we are going to start with roleplay in which you'll be given a case study and filmed with these actors before being critiqued by the rest of the class and rated on your individual performances."

And with that she produced a huge camera and instructed us to try and ascertain what was wrong with the second dog handler from The Bill, who had stepped away from the other actors and started flailing wildly.

"And you will start us off, David."

I spat my double mochaccino with an amaretto shot all down the front of my magenta tank top.

I am unclear about what happened next. All I know is that, ten minutes later, I was back in my chair, covered in sweat and trembling. Though I had not had one for many years, such absences had plagued me throughout school and appeared to be brought on by a combination of stress and tiredness. After zoning out for the entirety of a Home Economics lesson (and thus denying me the ability to make a Baked Bean Savoury for the rest of my life), my mum had finally decided to take me to see our crackpot GP.

After listening to my symptoms, she dashed off a prescription. "You're suffering from introspection, my love, take these."

I still do not know what the tablets were that she gave me but I took them fastidiously for two weeks. It was only years later, on discovering that introspection was a reflection upon one's emotional state rather than a medical condition, that I thought something was amiss. It was like when our friend Matt casually mentioned that his doctor had put his fingers up his anus when he had complained of a stiff neck and we had to gently tell him that this may not have been an entirely evidence-based intervention.

As happened at school, I eventually came back to my senses in the university hall and was relieved to find that my social work classmates were as nervous and inept as I was. Over the rest of the day we stuttered, stumbled and slurred our way through Mavis' cruel vignettes. An already tense atmosphere was further heightened by the seriousness with which the actors took it all, as Wayne was to find out to his cost when he tittered at a tense moment. The actress he was meant to be assessing for her life-threatening anorexia went mad at him for spoiling the scene – though it was noted in the canteen later that she wasn't completely committed to method acting as she happily wolfed down her lasagne, chips and beans.

This experience with actors made a big impression on me and so, when I was asked to act in a GP training day several years later, I readily volunteered. Me and my fellow thespians (most of the admin staff and the book club man) were put into separate rooms and asked to play a role which the medical students would take turns to try and diagnose. In room one I was to be their first case study, a suicidal milkman, and I poured my heart and soul into each performance (of which there were twenty-four). By the end of the day I was an empty shell. I'd given everything to the craft and the emotional intensity had left me drained. I had no more to give. As I staggered out of the door I noticed the pile of completed answer sheets lying on a desk and so I sneakily looked at the top one to see if they had identified my condition correctly.

It said gout.

Alongside the roleplaying, the course also required each student to complete a dissertation and my proposal sought to establish whether there was a correlation between the frequency of Mental Health Act assessments and the lunar calendar. I thought this would either prove or debunk a theory that most of my colleagues believed and, if true, would mean that I could tactically plan my annual leave to avoid the busiest times by booking holidays when there was a full moon. After much debate Mavis eventually turned my proposal down and I was left to explore something trivial like the use of violence against mental health patients in police custody.

For my work experience I was deposited in the cellar of a dilapidated Victorian mansion house where I was thrown into the daunting world of city centre mental health provision. I found the threshold for receiving a service to be alarmingly high and people who would raise serious concerns in the Home Counties would not get a sniff of Prozac here.

On my first day I was taken downstairs, briefly introduced to the team and left to fend for myself as frantic social workers on phones pushed me out of the way. Leafing through one of many overflowing trays that lay around the room, I found a completed Mental Health Act application. This was odd as, once completed, the form should be lodged with the hospital that the person had been admitted to. It was dated the previous week and so I asked the duty manager why it was there. She explained that the woman was at home and, despite lying in her own faeces with command hallucinations telling her to stab anyone that came near her, they had to wait for another three days until the police could support the ambulance to convey her to hospital. I was shocked by this – although the police I had liaised with in previous teams could be difficult and often required delicate negotiation, they would always come out on a call when needed. Here, if someone was of a mind to harm themselves or go on a drug-fuelled, shotgun rampage, they needed to wait until Thursday.

When Thursday came I accompanied the social worker and police to admit the distressed woman into hospital. From there I would go on to shadow a range of other assessments, always mindful (in the days before everyone was mindful) that time was literally (in the days before everyone misused literally) running out for me to front my own. Though I tried to avoid this for as long as possible, pressure from Mavis meant that I could not procrastinate indefinitely and so, one Monday morning, I resolved to take on the next assessment that came in.

Luckily, when the request came in, it appeared

straightforward. Mandy, a young woman with bipolar affective disorder whose section was due to run out later that day. The doctor who had been treating her felt that she needed to be in hospital for longer and, as she was keen to leave and felt that she did not need further treatment, he was requesting that his patient was assessed, with a view to placing her on a further section of the Mental Health Act to allow her to be held for longer. Because she was already in hospital there would be no need for police, no warrant to gain entry to her home, no ambulance, no conveyance; just reading through her notes, consulting with her Nearest Relative (who could block the section if they didn't agree) and arranging for two doctors to meet me on the ward.

When we arrived, the ward was chaotic with alarms going off and staff members looking stressed. There had just been an incident, a tired-looking nurse told us as she let us in, between two patients who both believed that they were Tupac Shakur.

"What are the chances of two Tupacs on the same ward?" I wondered aloud.

"More than you'd think," she replied, locking the door, "though it wasn't as bad as when we had two Gandhis in adjoining rooms last year – that got very nasty."

The assessing team were shown into a side room and Mandy was escorted in. I had spent the whole of the previous evening reviewing and re-reviewing the legal grounds for her detention. I had practiced how I would begin the interview, the questions I might ask and what the possible outcomes may be.

Mandy sat down and looked at me.

The nursing staff looked at me.

The two doctors looked at me.

I cleared my throat.

"Hello," I began, "we're here to undertake an assessment under the Mental Health Act. This follows concerns raised by your doctor who feels that, for your own health and safety, you need to spend more time in hospital. We're going to start by…yes?"

She had raised her hand.

"You always insist on peas and ketchup, don't you?"

"I beg your pardon?"

"You always insist on peas and ketchup, don't you?"

At midnight last night I had tried to visualise what direction the interview might take and anticipate any issues that may arise.

Would she ask to see my qualifications?

Would she challenge me on a legal issue?

Would she ask for a more experienced practitioner?

At no point had I prepared for being told that I always insisted on peas and ketchup.

She had thrown me a curveball and it had rattled me. "If we can start by looking at…"

"Admit it."

"Why you were brought…?"

"Admit it!"

Everyone was looking at me.

I didn't know what to do.

Should I just agree that I did, in fact, always insist on peas and ketchup?

That felt like collusion.

But if I argued that I didn't always insist on peas and ketchup that would open up a whole new world of pain.

Of course, on reflection, the obvious response was to ask what the fuck is all this talk about ketchup and peas, but on my first ever fronted assessment it was hard to think straight.

I ploughed on. "Can you remember…?"

"You always,"

"What was happening…"

"Insist on,"

"At the time of…"

"Peas,"

"Your admission…"

"And ketchup,"

"To hospital?"

"Don't you?"

Eventually one of the doctors stepped in to save me. "Mandy, could you tell me what the medication you're taking is for?"

"Well," she said, moving closer, "they say it's because I'm not well but I know that they're trying to poison me because I know too much and it's probably the government that are…"

To complete the course, I had to visit Mandy after several months to see the impact that the decision to detain her had had upon her life. I contacted her, fully expecting to be told to piss off or to be given more condiment-related grief but, to my surprise, she was happy to meet at her home. I went and saw her and she told me that things were better – she had been out of hospital for several weeks, her mood had settled and she was feeling positive about the future. She had started seeing friends again and was hoping to go back to work soon. She still felt traumatised about what she had been through and terrified that she would become unwell again. The worst part of it, she told me, was the feeling that she was the only person that had been through such an experience; that she was weak and was in some way responsible for what had happened.

This sense of stigma was something I would hear time and time again. People felt that they were alone and that no one else had been through something similar because no one talked about it. This was best highlighted when I visited someone in their mid-terraced home who told me that they were abnormal because no one else they knew was mentally ill. Confidentiality prevented me from telling them that I had seen their neighbours, on both sides, in the last year.

I knew that compulsory detention didn't help everyone in the way that it had helped Mandy and on many occasions it made things worse. But knowing that it had done some good gave me the momentum to keep going. I completed the course and, with my Approved Social Worker award filed carefully between my toenail cutting and food hygiene certificates, I returned triumphantly to my team.

SIXTEEN

"**W**hy the fuck did he get the job?"

Though the manager's door was shut and I was three rooms away, I could hear it clear enough. So could the rest of the office.

Earlier that morning several of us had been interviewed for the post of Senior Practitioner, a much sought after position that a close friend of mine had had to step down from when she had developed a chronic and debilitating health condition.

I couldn't believe my luck!

With a new qualification and an increased sense of confidence I had promptly applied and it had just been announced that I was the successful candidate.

At least one of the team was not euphoric about the decision and was just advising the manager of this fact.

"It's a disgrace, that's what it is. A fucking disgrace."

The door opened and my disgruntled colleague stormed down the corridor, flashing me an angry glance as she passed. At least my training had provided me with the skills to reflect upon such reactions, to consider what they might represent for the individual and examine them in a non-judgemental way.

Stupid cow.

I felt that I had been successful in getting the Senior Practitioner's job because I had worked long hours, always been flexible, tried to be a team player and had calmly managed a demanding caseload.

Or, as one of my colleagues surmised, "It's because you're a white male."

Now that I had the job I was determined to show that I was up to it and began taking on many of the more complex cases.

Nick was one such case.

In his late twenties, Nick was a big fan of alternative music, enjoyed playing football and was a psychopath. This was official – he had scored seventeen out of eighteen on the psychopathy assessment rating scale and I think the only reason he didn't score a mark on the last question was because the assessor just wanted to get out of there. Long before I met him he had been sent to prison following his interrogation of a member of the public during a psychotic episode. Unconvinced that the farmer was telling the truth when he said he was not a member of the Giggleswick branch of the Illuminati, Nick had proceeded to cut the shape of a daddy longlegs (it was meant to be a spider) into his back. From prison he had been swiftly transferred to a secure hospital after he had stated on numerous occasions that the prison wardens were all members of a secret society and his cellmate was Baby Spice.

For a psychotic psychopath with a penchant for torture, I found Nick a pleasure to work with. I would drive him to various appointments and he would regale me with stories of his past criminal activities.

As a youngster he would knock on people's doors and ask them for directions. They would politely provide him with these, sometimes drawing maps on scraps of paper, before he would bid them farewell and steal their car. He would then drive around until he saw a hitchhiker.

"Where are you going, mate?" he would ask.

"Glasgow/London/Manchester," they would reply.

"Well, you're in luck. I'm going to Glasgow/London/Manchester!"

The blissfully unaware passenger would then be delivered to their location before Nick went out looking for his next companion. On one journey, when he was driving a stranger to Billericay, he was spotted by the police and a car chase ensued. Nick excitedly described how he had eventually lost his pursuers and how his passenger had screamed in terror as they flew out of the Dartford tunnel at one hundred and ten miles per hour.

Only once did I see any glimpse of Nick's psychopathic tendencies and this was when, on a journey to another appointment with the psychiatrist, I was talking to him about my favourite albums of all time.

"David," said Nick, midway through my emotional critique of Barbara Streisand's Guilty, "you say the same things on every trip. You're really boring."

Clearly this was evidence of the inadequate conscience development, persuasive pattern of disregard for the feelings of others and intolerance and rejection of social values that were characteristic of a psychopath.

It couldn't be that I was boring.

Our working relationship was to take further strain when I phoned him early one morning to remind him about an appointment the next day.

"So, you'll pick me up tomorrow?" Nick clarified.

"Yes," I said yawning.

"Right, see you then," he said, "bye."

"Bye," I replied, before accidentally adding, "love you."
There was a pause and he put the phone down.
We never spoke about it again.

Like Nick, Samir was seen as a tricky customer who had led the team on a merry dance for many years. Fuelled by ginger wine and living in his elderly mother's front room, he would phone health services on a daily basis to tell them that he was about to kill himself. Ambulances would be scrambled and police would rush to do welfare checks only to find Samir snoring peacefully in front of Richard and Judy. The drain on resources was huge and, despite numerous support workers, contracts and final warnings, he carried on regardless.

Having been allocated to work with Samir, I resolved to put a robust care plan into action at the first opportunity.

I was not to wait long.

A day after taking him onto my caseload, Samir was on the phone to our duty desk telling them he was going to take an overdose. With a support worker and drug and alcohol advisor in tow, I hot-footed it over to his house where his mum let us in.

"He's in bed," she said apologetically, ushering us into the front room.

We gathered around the foot of Samir's bed where he lay dozing.

I was undeterred.

"Now Samir," I began sternly, "this has got to stop. I understand that life is difficult for you at the moment but we have to look for a way to change things."

He didn't stir. I was unmoved.

"I'm going to go through a care plan that I've put together that I think will not only develop your independence but will also help those people around you."

I produced a document and turned to my colleagues. "I think Samir is listening and I think it's a good idea if we go through it with him."

I started to read through each point on the care plan. Somewhere around point fifteen the support worker interrupted me.

"I don't think he's breathing," she said.

"Neither do I," said the drug and alcohol worker, pushing past me to check for a pulse.

The paramedics arrived within minutes and confirmed that Samir was indeed not breathing and probably hadn't been for the last few hours. His mum sat down in shock, my colleagues hugged each other in distress and I was left wondering how I had just managed to review fourteen points of a care plan with a dead person.

If the cause of death of a person under the care of mental health services is uncertain, a coroner will open up an inquest in an attempt to establish what happened. Alongside this, the NHS will carry out their own investigation to see whether all the appropriate policies and procedures had been followed. Whilst these reviews can be essential for providing the family with closure and can identify important learning opportunities for the future, for the staff member involved they are often an ordeal. As I was examined in forensic detail about the morning of Samir's death and my role in it, I dreamily reminisced about the times when the worst thing that could happen at work was being flung out of a JCB scoop or contracting leptospirosis.

After your first experience of a coroner's court you were

scarred for life. Upon hearing of an untimely death your first response was grief, but this would quickly be replaced by worry about whether you had recorded their crisis plan correctly. I often wondered if, on stumbling upon a service user in cardiac arrest, my immediate reaction would be to administer CPR or to update their risk assessment. Such was the fear of failure to follow procedure correctly that warm, caring humans could become cold, callous machines. Once, when walking through the office I saw a colleague on the phone joyously punching his fist into the air.

"Natural causes!" he mouthed excitedly, having just found out that a person he had worked with for over ten years had died of a heart attack rather than a suspected overdose and therefore wouldn't need to be reviewed by the coroner.

SEVENTEEN

Unfortunately, it would not be long before death's icy fingers would come and tickle me once more.

The service that I worked for had received notification that a Social Care inspection was due to take place and had been warned which of the cases were going to be audited. These inspections occurred on an annual basis and plenty of advanced notice was given to ensure that the inspectors were never exposed to the true chaos of mental health services. One of the service users they would be focussing on was Michelle, a woman for whom there were various safeguarding concerns which higher management felt hadn't been addressed properly. I was asked to review the case and follow up any actions that may have been missed. I had three days to do it before the inspection commenced.

A close examination of the files showed that there were various areas that needed attention. Most notable was a safeguarding concern that had been raised following Michelle's spontaneous decision last year to fund a fortnight's holiday for her and the staff at her private care home (who all came from a small coastal village in the Philippines), to a small coastal village in the Philippines. Nothing had been done to ascertain whether this was financial exploitation (it was – Michelle had stayed inside for two weeks as she suffered from prickly heat whilst the staff partied with friends and family) and so I set about writing up notes, completing forms and scheduling meetings. So immersed in the task did I become that it was only on the afternoon before the inspection that I went to meet with Michelle and introduce myself. I explained my role, why I had become involved in her care and how we would work together to ensure that she remained safe.

As I left she died of a heart attack.

The next morning I was scheduled to see the service manager so that I could give her an update on all the work that I had done prior to the Social Care inspection starting later that day.

"Oh Jesus," she said, after I had told her that the person she had entrusted me to safeguard on Monday was dead by Wednesday, "Oh Jesus, oh Jesus, oh Jesus."

As she sat with her head in her hands I quietly placed Michelle's (immaculately alphabetised) file on her desk and slowly retreated out of the office.

In order to survive such incidents, you needed a strong team around you and, apart from the small but significant group that despised me and my newly-purchased leather briefcase, I felt that I had this. My colleagues (not the ones that wanted me dead) and I recognised the importance of good teamwork in maintaining our sanity and so, alongside the daily discussions, weekly meetings and monthly training sessions, we would always get together once a year for a team building day.

I loved these days and would spend weeks organising them.

Whilst people's benefit applications remained blank, mental health unmonitored and medication uncollected,

I would be meticulously planning a scenario in which team members had to choose the five most important bits of equipment needed for a crash landing on the moon. Some years were more successful than others. My idea for everyone to pick a country at random from my lucky hat and come dressed in its national dress was ambitious. I had congratulated Dawn on her Mongolian peasant's costume only to be sharply told that she hadn't been aware it was fancy dress.

Perhaps I enjoyed these days too much and got lost in the occasion. Towards the end of my time with the team I received an anonymous note to ask whether we could use the upcoming away day to focus upon important clinical issues rather than another of my silly games. I was shocked and dismayed by such an assumption and briefly considered throwing away the one hundred and forty-four paper cups I had spent the last two hours labelling in preparation for Name That Crisp.

"David, you like this sort of thing."

My manager handed me a flyer announcing that the council had relaunched its historic Pancake Day race to raise publicity for the town and they were looking for teams to take part. I snatched it out of her hand, phoned a client to tell them they would now have to make their own way to the hospital for their double hip operation and started to assemble a team.

The day of the race arrived and I, along with my three carefully selected colleagues (the only three healthcare staff I knew who might survive a short burst of physical activity), presented ourselves at the registration point in the town centre. The high street had been closed off and crowds lined the course. We were shown to our lane and solemnly presented with a frying pan and pancake. It started to rain. As the other competitors started doing stretches my teammates stood around having a fag. The other teams wore lycra, gel trainers and breathable running tops. We wore faded Spastic Society t-shirts that our OT had found at the back of her cupboard.

We needn't have worried too much about our physical condition; an official on a public address system announced that due to the rain and the cobbles it would be walking only. The teams gathered at the starting line and waited for the starting pistol.

Donna, the twenty-a-day support worker, went off like a shot. She was followed by Justin, a trainee psychologist who kept up the pace but lost his pancake when he stumbled mid-flip and did his cruciate in. Stuart, our consultant psychiatrist, managed to make up the lost ground so that when I started the last leg I was neck-and-neck with the young child in the lane next to me. She was fast, focussed and seemingly unfazed by the wild elbow that I repeatedly threw in her direction to try and disrupt her pan-to-pancake coordination. As the finish line approached I abandoned all composure and legged it past her to snatch first place.

Though my rush of blood got the whole team disqualified there was no ill feeling. After the race we stood round helping ourselves to complimentary drinks and recounting the many highlights of the two-minute race. As we started to wander back to work a small chap in glasses sidled up to me and asked me what had happened at the event.

"I was disqualified from a race for running," I said and went home.

*

Later that evening I was called by my service manager. She had never called me at home and so I knew it was serious.

"What did you say to him?" she demanded.

I had no idea what she was talking about.

"I have no idea what you are talking about," I told her.

"The reporter. What did you say to him?"

I calmly reassured her that I hadn't said anything to any reporter. The only person I had spoken to was a small chap in glasses who had sidled up to me immediately after the event and written down everything I had said including my name and place of work from my identification badge.

"Oh," I said.

With a quiver in her voice, my service manager went on to tell me that the Trust's publicity officer had been contacted by four national newspapers to say that they would be running the story of the pancake race in tomorrow's edition. That it would focus upon the madness of health and safety and my disqualification and subsequent rage.

"The council will be furious with us," she said before putting the phone down.

I thought it was a joke.

"It's a joke," I said.

I was at my desk the next morning when the first national newspaper was brought to me.

HEALTH AND SAFETY RUINS PANCAKE DAY The Daily Mail.

Others soon followed.

FLOP ENDING TO RACE DAY The Mirror.

RUNNING BANNED IN PANCAKE RACE The Telegraph.

They were pinned to the window next to my desk and before long I was shrouded in darkness. In some of the articles I groaned, in others I poured scorn but mostly I flipped.

My quote was used to spearhead an attack upon the nanny state. It was discussed on GMTV, on the Conservative website and in The Washington Times. In The Orange County Register (circulation 340,000) the story was given greater prominence than articles on the Iranian nuclear threat and a paedophile being employed as a tour guide in a California theme park.

But, most ominously of all, was an embossed letter that I received from the British Prime Minister which thanked me for writing and assuring me that he had passed it on to the relevant minister to take forward. Whilst it is always nice to hear from the P.M., I was slightly perturbed by this as I had no idea what he was going on about. I had written no letter, and certainly no letter to the leader of our nation.

Soon after, an equally lavish response from the relevant minister arrived outlining what their department intended to do to address the issues I'd raised. Helpfully, a copy of my original letter had been enclosed – a letter which looked like it had been scrawled in blood across a piece of pig flesh, filled with random capitals, punctuation and wildly varying text size.

At the time, war was brewing in the Middle East, the Irish peace process was in the balance and the economy was slowing down and yet here was the government of the day spending a significant amount of energy responding to the deranged ramblings of a person purporting to be the Pancake Day One.

EIGHTEEN

Though my job was largely based in the community, I was often required to attend the local psychiatric hospital. Unlike other units I'd visited which tended to be crumbling away at the back of a general hospital, the one that served my team was a modern, purpose-built facility in the middle of the town. My friend lived around the corner from it and, not knowing its purpose but having seen many bewildered-looking people wandering in and out of it over the years, had always assumed it to be a teacher training college.

My first visit there came late at night after I had spent the whole day trying to convince one of the men that I worked with that he could really do with a short admission. I had been made aware of concerns about his mental health earlier that morning when the police contacted me to say that he had been repeatedly phoning 999 to report that his girlfriend had injured his penis during oral sex. By lunchtime he had been fired from his job as a lawn care sales representative for telling his customers that all they did was dump vast quantities of toxic chemicals over their garden and by the evening he was on the roof of his parent's garage in his underpants, refusing to come down.

After several hours of delicate negotiations I was eventually able to convince him that he needed to go into hospital (with the promise that his wounded dinky would be tended to) and so we agreed that I would escort him to the unit. On arrival, and in accordance with their policy, the staff took his bag off him to check that there was nothing prohibited in there. I felt confident there wasn't as, in the two hours I had waited outside his bedroom door whilst he had packed, I had made him aware of what he could and couldn't bring. The two nurses put on rubber gloves, carefully unzipped the huge suitcase and opened it up. Inside there were two Mr Kipling individual apple pies and a pair of swimming goggles.

Soon after this admission, I was asked (told) by my manager to start attending the weekly ward conferences at the hospital on behalf of the team. This was something I was not keen on because I had had to go to them as a student and was troubled by their archaic, stifling formality. Somewhere between a witch trial and the hokey cokey, patients would be deposited in the centre of a circle of strangers who drank tea, ate biscuits and made judgements. After being thanked for coming (they had no choice if they ever wanted to leave the hospital) the person would then be bombarded with the names and job titles of the fourteen people in the room before being asked what impact the new medication was having on their ability to ejaculate.

The conferences were invariably led by a consultant psychiatrist unless they were away on training, on holiday or on trial, in which case their staff grade would fill in. Our newly qualified consultant, Dr Boleros, had started at the same time as me and I was initially impressed by his vigour, vim and sense of mischief.

On our first home visit together I suddenly realised that I didn't know the name of the person we were visiting.

"It's Titty," said Dr Boleros, "he's French. Titté."

"Mr Titté?" I asked as the man opened the door.

"No," he said puzzled, "it's Mr Jenkins."

Another time, a very scary man told us that, because of the erectile dysfunction it caused, he only took his medication sporadically.

"Willy nilly?" said Dr Boleros, casting me a glance.

Dr Boleros billed himself as a placebo consultant and once confided in me that, prior to every meeting he would have to attend, he would meticulously plan what he would do if a lion stormed the room.

Unfortunately, as the years rolled on, I was to witness Dr Boleros' mental unravelling, culminating in his leaving dinner where, ravaged by peptic ulcers and sleepless nights, he sat at the head of the table with eight breadsticks jammed up his nose.

"Excuse me," he asked a passing waitress, "may I have some more breadsticks?"

In the intervening years he was subjected to all manner of calamities; being assaulted by a one-armed bare-knuckled boxer whose ears whistled when he blew his nose, being cursed by a woman whose toes of her shoes became longer and curlier the more ill she got and being formally disciplined when he left a patient's highly confidential file in a café, only for it to be found by the patient's fiancé. But these were mere body blows in comparison to the knockout punch that he was to receive on his return from his annual summer holiday.

Just hours before he was due to be at the airport, he had been required to go out on an urgent Mental Health

Act assessment to see a woman who was thought to be experiencing a manic episode. With time and bed pressures hanging over them, the assessing team eventually decided that it would be in everyone's interest if she remained at home. The Crisis Team went back to the office and Dr Boleros went to Fuengirola.

Two weeks later, at six in the morning, there was a knock at my manager's front door. She opened it to find Dr Boleros, who lived two houses down from her, in shorts and a Hawaiian shirt.

"I'm really sorry to bother you," he said, "but I've just got back from holiday and, I know this is stupid, but, it's been niggling at the back of my mind and I wondered if, and you'll think I'm silly, but you know the woman I saw just before I went away, I wondered if she is ok?"

"She is..." my manager began, before having the unenviable task of telling him that unfortunately there were many others who weren't as, the day after the assessment had taken place, she had got into her car and driven across a local campsite, knocking down many of its holidaymakers.

The tan drained from him and he stood in silence, the only sound the popping of his peptic ulcers.

As well as sounding the death knell on Dr Boleros' career with us, this incident had a profound effect on the whole of the team.

Its impact on the woman concerned, however, was less obvious.

"The only thing I want to know," she said to me as she sat down at her discharge planning meeting several years later, "is when I'm going to get my bloomin' driving licence back?"

Dr Boleros was just one of a smattering of psychiatrists I was to work with during this time and I soon came to realise that the uniformity, discipline and rigor that inhabited other branches of medicine had sold up and gone on a long holiday from psychiatry.

A broken bone? High cholesterol? Genital warts?

There was a clear and established evidence base, diagnostic criteria and treatment plan to follow.

But the mind?

The mind invited (and was regularly visited by) a diverse range of opinion, conjecture, speculation and twaddle.

This was best captured by the experience of Jemima, a young woman I worked with who had developed a series of tics which were having a profound and debilitating impact upon her life. First she was seen by a psychiatrist with psychodynamic leanings.

"What do you think is causing it?" asked Jemima, after going through her life story for over an hour.

"I think it's the dogs in your basement barking."

"Pardon?"

"It's the dogs in your basement barking. We'll go into it in more detail in our next session."

Unfortunately there was not to be a next session as the doctor moved to another job and Jemima was left to walk her barking dogs alone. His replacement, a devotee of systems theory, asked Jemima's parents to accompany their daughter to the appointment.

"What do you think is causing it?" asked Jemima once more as she brought her well-rehearsed life story to a close.

"Mum?" asked the doctor.

"I've no idea," said Jemima's mum.

"No," he said, "you've misunderstood. You asked me what the cause is – it's Mum."

After the appointment had finished (three minutes after the doctor had accused her mum of being largely responsible for her involuntary whistles, gulps, parps and toots) Jemima was clear that she did not want to go back. Luckily, going back would not be an option as this doctor also moved to another job and Jemima would go on to be treated by a succession of locums.

The first of these attributed her problems to a lack of vitamin C and promptly issued her with a prescription for 1000mcg morning, noon and night. It did nothing for her tics but after a month she had ultra-thermal night vision and urine like a lightsabre.

The second locum felt that the answer lay in cod liver oil and made poor Jemima chomp down tablets the size of beach balls for the next two months, at the end of which, she had skin like a supermodel but continued to bark when stressed.

The next one was warm and attentive and promised Jemima that he would apply a holistic approach to her problems. We could only speculate whether or not this would have worked, however, because he was shortly fired from his post for spending the night in one of the clinic rooms. Jemima was dismayed by this news although I wasn't completely surprised – one morning I had come in early to catch up on my work, only to find him bollock-naked, shaving in the large meeting room.

Eventually, a permanent psychiatrist was appointed who had a love of all things empirical and, over the following months, he proceeded to work through a plethora of checklists, worksheets, assessments, evaluations, inventories and rating scales with Jemima. Once completed the results were collated, analysed and reviewed before he called Jemima in and advised her that she was probably best to Google the condition herself.

This was the final straw for Jemima (who promptly moved to East Anglia where spontaneous shrieks were par for the course) and confirmed my distrust of checklists and rating scales which were being pushed as an alternative to the hunches, feelings, instincts and premonitions that pervaded psychiatry. I was regularly told to use them though I tried hard to resist since, already in my short career, I had seen how they could cloud judgement and become a distraction from the reality of the situation. On a visit to a young man who was felt to be going high, I was interrupted in the completion of my Longitudinal Rating Scale of the Manic State (which was indicating that everything was fine) by a knock on the door. The young man (who had just scored himself as a zero on disinhibited behaviour) sprang up and answered it. It was a courier delivering two life-size papier-mâché giraffes' heads (and necks) that he had ordered on special delivery in the early hours of the morning.

To poke the concept of applying binary measurements to emotional distress in the eye, I eventually decided that I would employ my own ratings systems and so, after giving careful consideration to a person's social context, I would provide them with their own personalised scale. These included fruit, puddings and members of the 1982 Scotland

World Cup squad and could prove invaluable for assessing how somebody was doing. When a young girl told me she was "positively satsuma", I was thrilled, when a man was feeling "Spotted Dick", mildly concerned. And on the occasion that I was given a message to say that someone I worked with was "close to Willie Miller", I phoned the crisis team immediately and reserved a hospital bed.

NINETEEN

When I was fifteen, I was in my bedroom when my mum and dad returned from a visit to the doctors. I went down to say hello and it was immediately clear that my dad had been crying. This was something that I'd only seen once before. On that occasion he had manhandled a bottle of his homebrew and, in agitating its highly unstable contents, had set off a chain of events that culminated in the cork firing into his eye. I knew therefore, that something very bad must have happened but, in keeping with my family's style of communication, I didn't ask and I wasn't told.

Later in the day I noticed that my sister had also been crying and, catching my puzzled expression, she told me that Mum had been diagnosed with cancer and was going to die. Until that moment the greatest loss I had had to endure was when Cagney the hamster had eaten the lower half of Lacey and so I was unsure what I should do next. Eventually, (and setting the pattern for all my future responses to stress) I had a bath, during which I decided that I was not going to think about my mum's illness ever again.

I made a conscious decision to slam the door shut.

There were some advantages to this tactic and, over the following year, I felt comfortably buffered from the horrors of terminal lung cancer. The drawback to such an approach, however, came after her death when I found that I was unable to access any memories, good or bad, that involved my mum. I looked at photos, home videos and her handbag in the airing cupboard (packed full of unsmoked Benson and Hedges) but to no avail. I even started psychotherapy but this naturally ended up with me talking about sex – particularly a dream I had had in which my genitals were bitten off by a vagina with gnashing teeth.

"A penis fly trap?" the therapist ventured, and this alone was worth the vast amounts of money I had paid him.

But it didn't help me remember my mum.

I thought a lot about my decision in the bath when I started working with Abdul, a man who was convinced that he was going to be abducted by aliens. Struggling to cope with the anxiety that this was causing him, he had confided in his colleague, who had confided in his manager, who had confided in his GP, who had confided in our duty worker, who had confided in me. I met with Abdul who, after considerable encouragement, agreed to start seeing me to explore some of these ideas in more detail. Unfortunately, this was never to happen as, hours after our first session had finished, he tried to take his life with a kitchen knife. He was swiftly admitted to hospital where, after several weeks, he was eventually allowed to go out on leave provided he did not go near sharp kitchen implements. True to his word, Abdul was soon brought back after trying to harm himself with a hammer.

And then a razor blade.

And then a drill.

In hospital, Abdul had been tried on all manner of antipsychotics which had brought him all sorts of side effects but little relief from the delusions. They had caused him to become restless, stiff, gain weight, have headaches and dribble, but had minimal impact on reducing his distress. This lack of a response to medication, together with an absence of accompanying symptoms, caused confusion as to the possible cause of his psychosis. To try and assist in this assessment process I was asked to meet with his wife to gather more collateral information. Over successive weeks, we would speak about Abdul's early childhood, his character, friends and family. It was during one of these meetings that she told me about their recent discovery that she had motor neurone disease, a condition that would ultimately lead to her death.

Central to Abdul's delusions was the belief that his house had been placed under surveillance, with the result that he felt unable to go home. With all attempts to discharge him ending with him acquiring sharp implements and involving the emergency services, there was no way of getting him safely out of hospital and he was to remain cocooned on the ward for years. In that time I was to hear various hypotheses advanced on what the underlying cause of the problem might be, from Asperger's Syndrome to alcohol, attention-seeking to an active imagination. But, although I found it hard to verbalise publicly, I felt confident that Abdul, like me, had chosen to slam the door shut (albeit with the addition of a few more padlocks, deadbolts, chains and panic alarms).

Abdul was eventually diagnosed with dissociative conversion disorder, a nebulous label plucked from psychiatry's equally nebulous diagnostic manual, the ICD-10. Like rating scales, the ICD-10 sought to bring the impression of understanding to an essentially incomprehensible aspect of the human condition by producing an exhaustive classification system for mental health. Whilst I struggled to understand the unique, nuanced experiences of the small number of people I worked with, the ICD-10 attempted to categorise on a global scale (and did so with gusto). Organic dysfunction, delirium, dementia, schizophrenia, schizotypal, schizoaffective, delusional, depression, bipolar, dissociative, phobic, anxiety, obsessive, neurotic and behavioural were all defined and detailed within the lengthy tome.

And these were just the headliners.

If you went off-piste and strayed into the subcategories you could find such gems as lack of leisure, discord with counsellor, intentional self-harm by hot vapour and adequate bowel control with normal faeces deposited in inappropriate places (we've all been there).

Alongside this myriad of diagnoses sat a multitude of syndromes which took things to a new level altogether; foreign accent syndrome, walking corpse syndrome, alien hand syndrome and genital retraction syndrome, to name but a few. They sounded so glamorous and I longed to experience them all (on other people) but, apart from one case of zoophilia (a man I saw on duty who regularly made love to his horse and proudly showed me photos of the miserable-looking creature), I never did.

Of all the diagnoses I encountered, by far the bleakest was inadequate personality disorder and the thought of giving this label to someone who, as the name suggests, may not be best equipped to deal with the news, seemed extremely harsh. Thankfully it has now been dispensed with but I was once copied into an initial assessment letter a psychiatrist had written to one of the people I worked with in which they concluded that they were clearly suffering from an inadequate personality disorder.

Fearing his reaction to this brutal news I rushed over to see him.

"I don't think it's right that they can say this after just one meeting," I said, trying desperately to reassure him.

"Well, they're the professional," he sighed inadequately.

Another man I met with this diagnosis would spend the majority of our meetings (which he timed on a little gold carriage clock to ensure that he got his full forty-five minutes) bemoaning the unreliability of the train service he used each day. Always one to grumble, but never to do anything about it, he eventually became so incensed by their continued lateness that he wrote a letter of complaint to the Chief Executive of the train company. Almost immediately after posting it, he started to regret what he had done. He was not used to such shows of assertiveness and became obsessed with the possible consequences of his actions.

What if the driver got fired?

What if the driver had a young family?

What if the driver came looking for him?

What if the driver found him?

What if the driver beat him to death with his little gold carriage clock?

From the minute he woke up to the minute he went to sleep, he thought of little else.

And then it stopped him sleeping.

He would pace his home into the early hours of the morning wishing he had not sent the letter. Eventually, tearful, exhausted and unable to think straight he decided that he could not go on and that the only option available was to kill himself.

"And what stopped you from doing it?" I asked, as he later recounted the tale to me.

"I was going to throw myself in front of a train," he replied, "but it was so late I decided not to bother."

TWENTY

I was always a big fan of making hoax calls to the duty desk, particularly at 5pm when the exhausted, emotionally-spent worker was getting ready to leave.

So when, at one minute to five on a day I was covering duty, I received a call demanding a Mental Health Act assessment, I was naturally suspicious.

"I'm the GP for this young man," lied the imposter, "and you need to see him immediately."

I scanned the office to try and find the culprit.

"He's been using crack cocaine and is adamant that he's going to kill himself."

I tried in vain to recognise the voice – probably a hanky over the phone.

"There are also huge risks to his physical health which I…"

"Alright, who is this?" I interrupted.

"Excuse me?"

"Come on wise guy!"

"Excuse me?"

It suddenly occurred to me that this may not be a prank after all.

"Look," continued Dr Gilbert (for it was he), "I'm still at the address and I'll wait for you but be quick!"

Having established that this was indeed a request for a Mental Health Act assessment at one minute to five on a day I was covering duty, I immediately phoned our Principle Officer to see if there was any way I could dodge this bullet. The Principle Officer was employed to provide advice and support to the Approved Social Workers. Our Officer was Clive, an omnipotent being who was always available and always knew the answer. He was like Yoda (if Yoda had resigned his post as Grand Master of the Jedi High Council, bought a battered Austin Allegro and gone to work in the social services department of the local authority). I had first met him at a meeting in which an array of senior managers proposed various solutions to an ongoing problem about hospital admissions. After half an hour Clive, who had remained silent throughout, was asked for his thoughts.

"Well, your suggestions are interesting," he told the assembled suits, "but unfortunately I am yet to hear one that is legal."

Legal they are not.

Years later, Clive retired and a dinner was held in his honour. Midway through his leaving speech his phone rang. It would be the last call he answered as Principle Officer and it was me, asking what I should do now that a manic policeman I had just sectioned had run out of his house, jumped on his daughter's trampoline and bounced over the back fence into the woods beyond.

Then, as now, I looked to Clive for the answer.

Then, he had told me to go home and leave it to others.

Now, I was hoping for similar advice.

"It's straightforward," he said, after I had carefully explained the situation, placing particular emphasis on the time of Dr Gilbert's request and the involvement of crack cocaine, "you've just got to go out and do it."

Once I had recovered from this bombshell, my first task was to find Dr McMorrin, our team consultant, and see if she would come out with me.

I approached her door gingerly. Dr McMorrin was a brilliant doctor but prone to fury. She would often become so annoyed with people that she would jump up and down on the spot like Rumpelstiltskin. We were once scheduled to attend a meeting with the gypsy liaison nurse so that we could build better links with people from this community. Dr McMorrin was running late and, as we waited, the nurse gave me an impassioned overview of the rich history of the gypsies and the terrible stigma and discrimination that they faced on a daily basis. As she finished, the door burst open and Dr McMorrin marched in.

"My first question," she said pulling up a chair, "is can we still call them tinkers?"

Luckily Dr McMorrin was still in her room when I knocked.

Luckier still, she agreed to accompany me on the assessment.

I was touched by this act of kindness because, not only would it certainly be a late one and she had no obligation to attend, but, on the last Mental Health Act assessment we had gone out on together, we had been savaged by the staff of a pub when we had detained their longest-serving regular.

"Bloody Big Brother," they had muttered as we took the man, and the large collection of Nepalese paperweights that he carried around with him, away.

Conscious of Dr Gilbert's impatience, I quickly filled

her in with all of the details as she grabbed her bag. I grabbed a handful of pink papers and we sped to the house.

When we arrived a group of anxious police officers were standing outside whilst inside a shaven-headed, tattooed death-machine screamed at a lump on the bed. The lump was our suicidal crack user.

"Just leave me alone," came a moan from within the sheets.

"I ain't fucking leaving you, Barry!" said the tattooed death-machine.

"But I just wanna die. If I can't 'ave Suzy, there's no point to any of it."

Suzy was nowhere to be seen.

Looking at the filthy pots, soiled clothes and sticky carpets, she had been gone for a while or, if she had just left, Suzy had made a dirty protest.

"You're here," said Dr Gilbert, stepping out of the shadows and peeling some used toilet roll from the sole of his shoe. "Now, can we get started?"

It didn't take long for the three of us to agree that Barry needed to be in hospital. Unfortunately for me, because of his fragile physical health, I would need to get him checked out in a general hospital before admitting him to a psychiatric ward. This was notoriously difficult and time consuming and it was already getting late. Having handed me their completed paperwork, the doctors made to leave. Since I would be staying, Dr McMorrin would need a lift back.

"Sorry," said Dr Gilbert, sounding very un-sorry, "but I'm going the other way."

"I'll take you," said the tattooed death-machine.

Before she had a chance to object, Dr McMorrin was being bundled into the back of his dilapidated jeep.

A police officer sidled up to me. "That's probably the most dangerous man in England," he said as we watched our consultant (possibly for the last time) head off into the sunset.

Whenever possible people are conveyed to hospital in an ambulance. If they refuse or resist, the police are used. Through a combination of ambulance staff, police officers and a very tight blanket Barry was escorted into a police van and conveyed to A&E where I explained the urgency of the situation to the nurse in charge. She told us to sit and wait.

"For how long?" I asked.

She gestured towards a large clock on the wall which announced that the current waiting time was two and a half hours. The police officers took Barry to the corner of the room and sat him down.

"Right, sir," said one of the officers turning to me, "we'll be off now."

Barry's eyes lit up.

"But can you not stay?" I asked, taken aback.

The officer looked pointedly at the waiting time. "Unfortunately, we have other calls to attend."

By now Barry was rubbing his hands.

"What if he runs off?" I whispered anxiously.

"Then just call us back," he said, before they disappeared out of the door.

The police van was barely out of the carpark when Barry ran off. As instructed, I phoned the police and was told that all the officers were currently busy but they would get someone to me as soon as possible.

An hour later the same officers returned and told me that there wasn't much they could do but they'd have a drive round to see if they could see him.

Half an hour later they brought Barry back and deposited him in his seat.

"Now stay there," they said to him sternly.

Barry looked at me sheepishly.

The police started to leave.

"But you can't go," I panicked, "he'll just run off again."

"Then you'll need to call us back. Good luck."

I rushed over to the nurse in charge and asked how much longer.

"Two and a half hours," she grunted.

"But we've been here for nearly two hours!"

"He left – the clock restarts."

I turned, dejected, only to see Barry scuttling out of the exit. The automatic doors closed behind him. As I reached for the phone to call the police back the doors reopened and the death-machine strode in, carrying Barry like a babe-in-arms.

I could have kissed his tattooed lips.

"Barry's going to wait with me in my jeep," he told me.

Deprivation of liberty is a complex issue with lots of nuances and avenues for interpretation. Keeping someone in your jeep against their will was not ambiguous; it was kidnap. I decided to stay in the waiting room and watch the clock rather than the unlawful imprisonment going on in the carpark. Eventually the nurse called Barry's name and we quickly brought him to the bay so that his clock would not be restarted. After three hours of waiting, chasing, catching and keeping Barry captive, it took twenty minutes to give him the medical all-clear.

My next challenge was to get Barry from the general hospital to the secure psychiatric ward some twenty miles away. This would need the police again and so I called and requested their attendance. Linda, the police telephone receptionist who I was now on first name terms with, told me that they would be there as soon as possible. As I was making these arrangements, a scene was developing outside. A woman had turned up to tell the death-machine that he needed to come home with her. Death machine had agreed and instructed a sobbing Barry not to move a fucking inch.

As I came out of A&E into the cold night air I saw death-machine and Suzy (for it was she) driving off in one direction and Barry legging it into the other.

It was now 2:00 a.m.

I had been working for seventeen hours.

I was tearful and starting to hallucinate. I thought a tree in the distance was a Tyrannosaurus Rex.

I should have updated the police and gone home.

Left it to others.

But I didn't.

Instead, something inside me snapped and I started to chase Barry through the deserted streets. Along roads, over bridges, across roundabouts we puffed and panted. I hadn't run so hard since Pancake Day and it was doubtful that Barry had done any physical exercise in this millennium. Yet no matter how hard I pushed myself, he always remained just out of reach.

I was doubled up, dry retching on a street corner when the police van pulled up beside me.

I pointed breathlessly.

"Barry…" I wheezed, pointing at the figure in front, "… get him."

At 3.30 a.m. I finally checked Barry into the secure psychiatric ward. As I did a handover, glossing over the more illegal parts of the day, the telephone rang. The nurse answered it.

"It's for you," she said, puzzled.

I took the phone apprehensively.

It was 3.30 a.m. In my deluded state of mind this could have been anyone.

Tupac?

Gandhi?

Titsy?

"Hello?" I said.

It was Clive, just checking I was okay.

TWENTY-ONE

I bumped into Barry several months later, looking smart and well.

"That was some night," I said, unsure if he even remembered it.

"Pure madness," he said, shaking his head.

We stood awkwardly for a few moments.

"Saved my life though," he mumbled and walked away.

Not everyone was as positive as Barry about their experiences under the Mental Health Act and as I did more and more assessments the list of people who wanted to assault me grew longer and longer.

Top of this list was a famous actress who had recently moved into a hotel room in our team's catchment area. We had received a referral from Children's Services to inform us of this and to report their concerns about her mental health. Over the previous year the actress had developed a belief that she was in a relationship with another member of the film industry. She was making repeated contacts with him, posting updates on her website and had recently changed her youngest child's surname to his last name. He had reported this to the police, saying that he did not know her, and their inquiries, together with the investigations of social services, confirmed this. Concerns about the psychological impact upon her child had led to him being placed under the care of his father whilst help was sought for the mother.

My initial attempts to make contact with the actress were a failure and my offers to meet up were flatly ignored. Over the following weeks I sent her appointment after appointment but she would not come out of her room. Things became more urgent when Children's Services informed me that they intended to go to court to apply for a care order for her youngest son. There was now a real risk that she would lose custody of her child as a result of her mental health difficulties and so a more assertive intervention was needed. I wrote to her again to stress the importance of meeting up and the potential consequences of not doing but still she declined to see me. After long discussions with my colleagues it was agreed that we would look at undertaking a Mental Health Act assessment.

As we would require access to the actress's room, I contacted the manager of the hotel and gave her a brief overview of the situation. The manager was rightly protective of her guest's privacy and told me that I would need to get a warrant to gain entry. The following day I attended court, waited three hours in a cold side room, swore an oath I didn't believe in and presented my case to the magistrate.

I told her the name of the hotel.

"And which room number do you require the warrant for?" she asked.

I was unaware that you were unable to get a warrant to search an entire hotel – just a single room. I was also unaware of which room the actress was in.

I returned the following day having found out the room

number and, after waiting three hours in a cold side room, swearing an oath I still didn't believe in and presenting my case to the magistrate, I was able to get the warrant.

One of the central principles of the Mental Health Act is to treat people equally and, though I always tried my best to do this, when you're driving to see someone and their latest performance is being lauded on Radio Four, it can be hard. Fearful of high-powered lawyers and media interest, I exhausted myself making sure that everything was done perfectly. As everyone else slept I would check and recheck each point to ensure that no mistakes were made.

The correct identification of the actress's Nearest Relative was one area which I pored over for hours. The role of the Nearest Relative is central to the Mental Health Act. They have the power to request discharge, prevent treatment and can even compulsorily detain their relative in hospital. It is essential therefore to identify them correctly and make them aware of their powers and responsibilities. The Act sets out an order of primacy for determining the Nearest Relative which begins with their partner and ends with more distant relations.

I started to work through the list.

As she currently had no partner (though she would strongly contest this) the next people to consider were her children. A Nearest Relative cannot be under eighteen and so her two children, aged four and seventeen, were disregarded. Parents were next and, as her father was the eldest, he would be the Nearest Relative.

Prior to commencing a Mental Health Act assessment, it is a legal requirement to consult the Nearest Relative and case law is littered with accounts of judges flaying social workers who had decided not to. I was keen to avoid this and, after considerable effort, I managed to track down the actress's father and speak with him.

Once this had been done, the assessment could proceed and so I set out for the hotel with two doctors and a warrant.

On arrival, the manager took us to the actress's room and, after I explained the situation through the door, she reluctantly let us in.

She was not happy to see me.

"Do you know who I am?" she said, flinging one of her DVDs at my head.

"I do," I said, ducking.

"Well you need to be quick. I'm due to be meeting my son in a bit for his eighteenth birthday."

I apologised but continued. It was only when I had finished introducing the doctors that the relevance of her son's eighteenth birthday hit me.

Oh fuck.

As well as becoming an adult he also now took on the unwelcome responsibility of becoming his mum's Nearest Relative.

I hadn't consulted with him and so the assessment couldn't go ahead.

We slunk out of the hotel.

Several days later I managed to speak to her son, go to court again, wait for three hours in a cold side room, swear an oath I was now starting to believe in, present my case to the magistrate, get a warrant, assess the actress and admit her to hospital.

In the weeks which followed, her anger towards me intensified and I became the focus of her rage. I would arrive at my desk each morning to find my answer machine flashing at me.

"This is a message for Mr I-Don't-Know-You-From-a-Bar-of-Soap," it would begin, "now let me tell you…"

It would only end when the memory was full.

Mr I-Don't-Know-You-From-a-Bar-of-Soap was one of the least offensive names I was called.

You cunt was the most common, closely followed by you fucking cunt.

I once assessed a very well-to-do wheelchair-bound old lady who had dementia. I sat down at her level so as not to intimidate her and tried in my most gentle voice to explain why we were worried about her.

"Get swizzled!" she replied.

I was gobsmacked.

Another time I went and saw someone on the ward with a view to extending the length of their detention. I walked into the busy television lounge, wearing glasses and a scarf, to ask him to come to a quieter room.

"Oh, Jesus Christ," he said loudly, "I'm going to be sectioned by Harry fucking Potter!"

The most public abuse I received was delivered by Mrs Henderson, an elderly lady who was suffering from a psychosomatic illness which was causing her to call an ambulance several times a day. Meetings between the emergency services, her GP and our team had not been able to resolve the problem and so a hospital admission was being considered to see whether it would alleviate Mrs Henderson's distress. I was explaining this to her at her front door when she suddenly bolted past me and flagged down a passing bus. It stopped and she jumped on.

"This rapist!" she shouted at the bewildered passengers whilst pointing at me, "this rapist is trying to take me away! Will somebody please help me?"

Luckily nobody did, though someone recognised me years later.

"Oh," they said, as I picked my child up from the nursery, "you were the rapist on the bus."

TWENTY-TWO

A longside verbal abuse, I regularly encountered physical aggression, particularly in the fraught atmosphere of a Mental Health Act assessment where people were often scared, tense and unpredictable.

One cold winter's evening, I found myself driving around a housing estate desperately trying to find Charlotte, a heavily pregnant woman with a diagnosis of schizophrenia who was, according to her husband, becoming unwell again. I searched for the tell-tale signs of an imminent Mental Health Act assessment: doctors standing idly around, neighbours peering through their net curtains, Radiohead playing, vultures circling.

Eventually I spotted a woman outside a large block of flats, with a mop and bucket, furiously washing the pavement.

Charlotte.

I pulled up and tried to introduce myself but, on hearing the words social worker, she promptly disappeared into her home and slammed the door shut, leaving me to wait on the (spotless) pavement outside.

Eventually the two doctors joined me and we went to Charlotte's door to try and convince her to let us in. After several minutes of negotiating through the letter box, half-expecting a mop handle to poke out and jab me in the eye, the door swung open and we were ordered to take off our shoes and go into the front room.

Things started well and we talked about the concerns that had been raised and the types of support that might be appropriate during this difficult time. As I gently raised the possibility of hospital admission Charlotte jumped up.

"Stay there!" she shouted, and ran out of the room.

We looked at each other nervously.

Charlotte returned with a battered canvas satchel and walked up to one of the doctors.

"This…is…for…you!" she said, furiously rummaging through her bag.

In those tense moments I tried to anticipate what she would pull out.

A knife?

A gun?

Blow torch and pliers?

It turned out to be far more disturbing; a stained ceramic mug with a faded photograph of her long dead cocker spaniel on it.

"See?" she said, thrusting it towards one of the doctors, "see?"

He nodded quickly.

"Now, wait there!"

She rushed into the other room again.

As one we ran out of the door in our socks and phoned for the police.

It was dark by the time the police arrived and, after giving them an overview of the situation, they agreed to accompany us into the flat. Nervously, I knocked on the front door.

"Oh hello," said Charlotte warmly, as though her earlier threatening use of pottery had never occurred, "come in, come in!"

The two doctors, two police officers and I funnelled into the front room and returned to the subject of what support Charlotte might need.

She managed to hold it together for three seconds.

Springing to her feet, she pushed past the policemen and ran into the other room. They followed her whilst the doctors and I stood quietly, listening to the drama unfold.

"Let's go back, Charlotte."

"Wait!"

"Try and keep calm."

"Don't come near me!"

"Now leave that alone."

"Get back!"

"What is it?"

"Don't touch me!"

"Put that down."

"Give that to me."

"Go and speak to the doctors."

"Come back!"

Suddenly Charlotte, wielding a sink plunger and pursued by the officers, charged back through the front room and out into the hallway. Before they had a chance to grab her she reached up to the fuse box and flicked the big red switch off. We were thrown into darkness.

Grabbing their torches and radioing for backup, the police desperately searched the flat trying to locate a very distressed pregnant woman armed with an implement for unblocking the u-bend whilst the doctors and I huddled together, straining eyes and ears for any clue as to where she might be. I tried to keep as quiet as possible but yelped when something brushed against my hand. The doctor beside me also yelped – it was his hand. Eventually a police officer found the fuse box, turned the light on and located Charlotte in the kitchen, crouching behind a pile of ironing.

When I returned to the office I had to record this incident as an alert on the front page of Charlotte's notes. Alerts were commonly used to share risks amongst staff and I would routinely check them before going out on a home visit.

Risks of aggression, allergies and self-harm were all commonly recorded but the one that I read prior to seeing a young man in a residential home will stay with me till the day I die.

DO NOT ALLOW TO WATCH THE NEVER ENDING STORY 2.

In quieter moments I found myself speculating on the reasons behind this alert.

Was it because the film was terrible?

Should I be doing this?

KEEP WELL AWAY FROM POLICE ACADEMY 7.

UNDER NO CIRCUMSTANCES EXPOSE TO BEVERLEY HILLS CHIHUAHUA.

Or was it because he hadn't seen the first one and they didn't want to spoil it?

I had intended to raise this with the staff on the assessment but was distracted when the young man in question had charged at me with a bread-bin.

Together with the use of alerts, teams also employed emergency codes to try and keep their staff safe. For the Community Mental Health Service, if I was at risk of being assaulted, abducted or generally interfered with, I was to phone the receptionist and tell her I've left the red file on my desk. For my Mental Health Act work I had to ask them to let Johnny know I am running late. For my previous teams, I'll pick up some milk on the way back and I'm going to be a while so water my plant had been dreamt up.

On paper the idea of a secret code seemed sound, but in practice it was a disaster and, with so many phrases rattling around my head, I was never far away from unwittingly triggering an armed response unit being scrambled. On the first occasion that I actually needed an armed response unit I was so stressed that I messed it up completely.

I was trapped in a consultation room with a violent Malteser (he was from Malta) and managed to convince him that I needed to use my phone. Under his menacing gaze, I tried in vain to summon up the phrase that would raise the alarm.

"I'll pick up the plant on the way in," I told our receptionist.

"I beg your pardon?"

"Urm... I've left the milk on my desk?"

"Sorry?"

"Water Johnny for me!"

"I'm going to put the phone down now."

The second time, when I had been taken hostage by a demented sailor who told me he was going to kick the baby out of my belly, I was sure to get it right.

"I've left the red file on my desk," I said loud and clear, "I've left the red file on my desk."

"Okay, but you're going to have to bear with me," said

the voice on the other end of the line, "I'm covering as the usual secretary is off sick."

And with that she wandered off to look for the red file.

TWENTY-THREE

The Capacity Act was introduced to support people in making decisions about their lives and, when they are unable to do this, provide a statutory framework for decisions to be made in their best interest. The Act is applied on a decision by decision basis rather than a person having, or not having, capacity and, if a person can be seen to retain, understand and weigh up the information relevant to a particular decision, they cannot be prevented from making it.

Even if it is unwise.

So, when one of the young women I worked with went to Glastonbury to sell five hundred grams of no-frills bicarbonate of soda to unsuspecting festival-goers she was fully aware of the risks and possible outcomes of this decision and could not be prevented from making it – despite it being unwise (an unwise decision that made her about £6,000).

But when I arrived at a man's house to find him having a barbecue in his front room, it was clear that he was unable to weigh up the information relevant to the decision (the thrill of smoky-tasting sausages set against the risk of burning down his mum's bungalow) and so I made a (hasty) best interest decision to fling the disposable barbecue out of his window.

*

Since I was already an Approved Social Worker when they introduced the Act, I was fast-tracked onto Capacity training and soon found myself being regularly consulted on its application. The first query I was to receive came from the local psychiatric hospital who wanted advice on a capacity issue that they were struggling with, and so I agreed to go over and discuss it with their intimidating and long-serving ward manager.

The manager and I had a difficult relationship which had seemed to start around the time she informed a packed ward conference that the reason the room was so cold was because they were dependent on an antiquated heating system. I had simply pointed out that we were well aware that the hospital was being run by an old boiler.

Tensions were increased further when, soon afterwards, I convinced her to allow one of my nice young chaps to have a bit of respite on her ward.

"As long as he doesn't cause any trouble," she warned.

"He won't," I assured her.

He did.

She was having a cup of tea and a biscuit in her office when the anti-terrorist officers arrived. They had just received information that a recent telephoned bomb hoax, which had resulted in a nearby supermarket being evacuated, had been traced to her office. Her phone was seized, my nice young chap later confessed and I was unable to get her to agree to respite ever again.

Following these incidents, I had been keen to try and make amends and so, on receiving her request for help with the Capacity Act, I immediately went over to the ward where she explained the situation to me.

A man had recently been admitted suffering with severe depression. There were concerns about his home situation; he lived with his elderly parents who felt that rather than antidepressants and visits from his nurse he just needed to pull his socks up and his finger out. With growing concern about his food and fluid intake the nurse had eventually arranged for him to be admitted into hospital. The man appeared to come willingly and it had not been felt necessary to use the powers of the Mental Health Act to detain him. However, the ward manager wanted my view on whether his admission was compliant with the Capacity Act.

After reading through all of his notes, I met with the man and concluded that, although he lacked the capacity to make the decision to come into hospital, it was in his best interests for him to do so and he appeared happy to remain. He attended groups, took his medication, chatted with other patients and made no attempt to leave. I completed the relevant paperwork and went merrily on my way.

I was on Traumatic Event Debrief training when I received a call from the hospital's legal department. I had gone to the training because I thought that, due to the nature of my work, any advice on how to cope with traumatic events would be most welcome. Ten minutes in and I realised that the course was for people to lead team debriefs rather than just attend them.

In America, where the intervention was pioneered, such a course would take a minimum of a year. In the NHS it was done on a Tuesday afternoon.

Feeling too self-conscious to admit my error, I decided

that I would stay for the duration. Besides, the skills might come in useful and it couldn't be worse than when I mistakenly signed up for the wrong first aid course and, instead of basic life support, I ended up having to inject rectal diazepam into a novelty plastic bottom.

(It was worse – within a month I was dispatched to debrief a team traumatised by the sudden death of their longest serving staff member.

"Tell me something about Betty," I asked the group tenderly.

"She was called Nancy," they replied.

I had gotten her name wrong.)

Over the phone, the solicitor explained that the parents of the man who was now in hospital had got legal representation to challenge my decision that being in hospital was in their son's best interest. This was not unusual, he assured me, particularly in the wake of new legislation, where uncertainties about an Act's interpretation exist. I understood this but was anxious to ensure that Emery vs the Nice Elderly Couple didn't become a defining piece of case law that people would quote for generations to come.

"You've done an Emery," they would say when a significant legal injustice had been committed.

"What you need to do," the solicitor instructed me, "is to section him under the Mental Health Act so that any issues about the application of the Capacity Act will become irrelevant."

One of the first things you are told when you train to become an Approved Social Worker is the importance of your independence. You alone are responsible for the decisions you make and the consequences of them. On the course, Mavis had sought to underline this point by telling us about the newly qualified worker who, whilst conveying someone to hospital, agreed to their request to stop at a garage for cigarettes. Having bought these, the person proceeded to grab a petrol pump from someone on the forecourt, douse themselves in petrol and light a match. The Approved Social Worker subsequently received counselling and their P45.

Another fresh-faced graduate, Mavis merrily recounted, was asked to assess Mr Smith, an eighty-six-year-old gentleman who was running amok in his local community. His exhausted daughter had told them of his propensity to go out immediately after breakfast and not return until it was dark and so the assessment was arranged early in the morning. When they arrived he was confused and disorientated and it did not take long to decide that he needed to be in hospital. Just as they were filling in the section papers his daughter phoned them to ask where they were as she had been waiting with her father for the last hour – they had gone to the wrong house and were a whisker away from sectioning Mr Smith's sleepy next door neighbour and losing their warrant forever.

Having read the Capacity Act in full, its Code of Practice and all the guidance available, I felt that my decision that admission was in his best interest was sound. I talked it through with Clive, who agreed.

That was enough for me.

I wasn't going to section someone just to avoid a day in court.

Why didn't I just section him to avoid a day in court?

I sat in the dock of the High Court, where killers,

rapists, paedophiles and Peter Andre had stood before me. I had no colleagues to support me, no mysterious girl to say everything would be okay. My earlier confidence had vanished and the only hope I clung to was that his parent's barrister had a fourth edition of the Mental Health Act manual whilst I had the twelfth edition.

Surely that counted for something?

The judge entered the court room; a judge whose rulings I had written lengthy essays about. I felt a bit starstruck – like when I bumped into the Krankies at a leisure centre in Watford.

I sombrely bowed my head (for the judge, not the Krankies).

The court had appointed an official solicitor to represent the man and she had spent time on the ward, prior to the case being heard. The official solicitor was asked to present her findings.

After much deliberation (and at £240 an hour, I too would have had much deliberation), she told us that she believed that the man needed to be in hospital (excellent), it was in his best interest to be there (fantastic) but he was not willingly staying there (bollocks).

I had therefore been complicit in the deprivation of his liberty.

As he met the criteria to be detained under the Mental Health Act, the judge surmised, this was the correct legal remedy and, twenty minutes later in a long draughty corridor, the one that I took.

By the end of the day, I had sectioned a man I hadn't wanted to section, the man who didn't want to be in hospital was in hospital, the parents who wanted him home didn't get him home, the hospital which had sought to act in a legal manner had acted illegally and the ward manager I had been trying hard to impress was unimpressed.

There were no two ways about it.

I had done an Emery.

TWENTY-FOUR

My first encounter with Advanced Statements came whilst trying to assess a man who was living on his parents' farm.

"He has an Advanced Statement," advised his mum, as she passed me a formal-looking piece of paper, "which states that under no circumstances should he be taken into hospital against his will."

Unfamiliar with this document, I was unsure whether such a request would apply to his current circumstance; namely, standing on top of the cattle shed in his pyjamas frisbeeing roof tiles at me. Luckily, after luring him off the roof with the promise of a supporting letter for his court appearance the next day, the man did not require hospital admission. He remained at home and I went off to find out about Advanced Statements.

Advanced Statements, I discovered, were legal documents in which people could record how they would like to be treated if they lost the capacity to make decisions for themselves. Though they are requests rather than demands, failure to consider them can result in censure. If a man had an Advanced Statement in place saying that, in the event of losing capacity, he should be allowed to have a barbeque in his front room, I would be legally required to read the statement, consider its implications and determine whether it was possible to adhere to it (before flinging it out of the window).

Despite their limitations, I could see how Advanced Statements might be used to give someone more control of their lives. They could record a person's views on which hospital they would like to go into, what to do with their finances, who should look after their pets and who should inherit their large collection of paperweights. If I was unfamiliar with them, it was likely that the people I worked with were also unaware of their existence and so I decided that I would arrange some training sessions to raise their profile.

There was a good response to the training and many of the people who attended saw the potential that they offered. This was highlighted by one quiet man on the front row who fastidiously took notes and at the end, came and told me that he intended to complete one that very evening.

My next encounter with Advanced Statements came as I was preparing to go out on a Mental Health Act assessment and was told that the person I would be assessing had one in place.

I found it in the front of his file and it said:

If I should become mentally unwell I would like the professionals that deal with me to be strict.

I was surprised by such a request and unsure of its legality. Whilst it was signed, dated and witnessed correctly I was uncertain whether instructing others on how to behave towards you fell within the realms of such a statement, particularly when asking someone who had spent a career cultivating wishy-washyness to suddenly become a dominatrix. I discussed it with the team and decided (in keeping with someone who had spent a career cultivating wishy-washyness) to try and be a little bit strict.

I arrived at his home with the rest of the assessing team

and knocked on the door only for it to swing immediately open. Standing behind was the quiet man on the front row from my Advanced Statement training session.

Except this time he wasn't quiet.

Dressed in nothing but a billowing silk kimono, his testicles angrily clanking together like ball bearings on string, he waved a rubber cigarette menacingly towards me.

"It's my fucking wife isn't it?" he shouted.

I had once been advised that if I showed no fear to a herd of cows they would not bother me. When I was little and being regularly terrorised by a Jack Russell on my paper round, I was told that if I looked him in the eye and raised myself up to my full height (3'4") I would be untroubled.

I had dutifully followed both pieces of advice: the dog had bitten me and the cows would have trampled me to death if I hadn't clambered onto a bale of hay.

There was no way I was going to be strict with this chap.

"Ever so sorry to have bothered you," I apologised, before later returning with four police officers and sectioning him from safely behind them.

Following this experience, I added Advanced Statements to my long list of things that I felt should have been covered on my social work training but weren't. Whilst I knew that there would always be a need for a theoretical understanding of sociological constructs and a sound knowledge of the psychological perspective on human development, I found both to be of little benefit when faced with, for example, a semi-naked man waving a rubber cigarette in anger. Stress management would have been more useful than the stress vulnerability model, self-defence preferable to self-reflection.

Similarly, I cannot recall one mention of medication over the whole two years of my course, but would spend a considerable amount of my working life dealing with pharmacological queries. On graduating, I knew nothing of antipsychotics, mood stabilisers or tranquilisers but soon realised that I would have to familiarise myself with them fast. Over time, I was able to come to understand dosages, interactions, contra-indications and side-effects enabling me to discuss the potential benefits of antidepressants with Wayne, who was strongly opposed to polluting his body with that shit (though he had no qualms about flooding his system with MDMA, speed and crack cocaine) and advise Tommy that taking his dog's diazepam was probably not the best idea – for him or his (increasingly anxious) Airedale Terrier.

I.T. was another area that proliferated my daily work but was scarcely mentioned during my training. Perhaps if I had had some lessons in computing I would not have had to make daily calls to our IT helpline to amend the mistakes I made in my electronic notes (such as when I typed that I had taken a full clitoral, rather than collateral, history). I was vaguely aware that my constant calls irked the computer technicians but received proof of this when our team were issued with a batch of user names for a new e-rostering system. My colleagues were HOLID4Y, SUMM3R and RA1NB0W.

I was W4NKER.

But a lack of training in IT and medication were mere oversights when compared to the course's most glaring omission; tea etiquette, an issue that every community-based healthcare professional had to negotiate every day, of every week, of every month of every year.

When I first qualified, I said yes to every cup I was offered, anxious not to offend anyone. Earl Grey from bone china, builder's from broken mugs, Lapsang with lemon, stewed brews with sludge – I accepted them all and many was the time when a floater of unknown origin would casually bump against my lip and I would be compelled to swallow it down wordlessly. For the first few years after qualification I was probably getting through twelve cups a day and my bladder and sleep pattern paid a heavy price.

One day, as I drove back to the office, I found that I had so much tea sloshing around inside me (after accepting a cup from each of my four morning visits), that I had to quickly pull over by the side of the road and dash into a nearby bush to relieve myself. Midway through, I looked up to see a large group of primary school children staring and pointing at me. I was urinating by a playground. With the muscle control of a ninja I instantly stemmed my flow and, with only a small wet patch on my crotch, fled from the scene, terrified that I would be in tomorrow's papers for exposing myself to the under seven community.

Something had to give and, on learning from a colleague that a patient I regularly took tea with had confessed to lacing her guests' hot beverages with her Hormone Replacement Therapy tablets, I decided that enough was enough.

I stopped everything.

Tea total.

And, although it was difficult to continually turn down people's kind offers every day, of every week, of every month of every year, my bladder soon recovered and my sleep pattern improved (though I did notice that, now HRT free, my hot flushes and erratic moods returned with a vengeance).

TWENTY-FIVE

Other than trying to dissuade a homicidal support worker from ordering a hit on her ex-husband, my previous experiences of management had not involved much management but rather, more bum-wiping only in slightly smarter trousers. Despite this, I enjoyed the increased independence and pay that a manager's role had brought me and, having worked as a senior practitioner in the Community Mental Health Service for several years, I felt that I was now ready to lead my own team. With social work managers always doing well in the professions with the highest rates of suicide charts (just behind farmers and dentists) I did not have to wait long.

Unlike the piecemeal services provided for people with a learning disability who had been cast out into the community when the institutions had closed, a substantial investment had been made to help people with mental health problems adapt to their new lives. The Home Support Team was central to this provision and was established to ensure a smooth transition from hospital to home. At its inception, it was composed of large numbers of social workers, nurses, occupational therapists and support workers but wave after wave of reviews, reorganisations and redundancies had decimated this once thriving team into a small band of six fiery, hard-core militants.

And they needed a manager.

My carefully completed application form, extensive research, detailed presentation at interview – and the fact that I was the only person who had applied – meant that I was successful in getting the job. On my first day I met with the service manager to go through what my priorities would be. There was only one, she told me, and it was a classic piece of fuckwittery that could only be found in the National Health Service.

A law had recently been passed that required all service users to be offered a personal budget. The philosophy behind personal budgets was sound: people were given access to funds, based upon their need, which could then be used to commission their own support. Rather than being limited to bingo and basket weaving at their local day centre, people could arrange personalised activities, such as gym membership and yoga groups, to improve their recovery. Unfortunately, the process for accessing personal budgets was a nightmare, with workers having to complete reams of paperwork, undertake complex calculations and have ongoing responsibility for monitoring to make sure that they were used correctly (it would only take one service user to use NHS funds to pay for cocaine and a prostitute for there to be a public outcry). As a result, very few people had a personal budget. This was relevant to the Home Support Team because it had been decided (days before I got the job) that this was a service that needed to be funded entirely by the personal budgets of those people who used it. If the team couldn't generate enough funding, I was told, it would close.

My first task was to meet with the team and explain the situation to them since no one else had thought to do so.

Like the messenger at the start of Gladiator, I was nearly returned to my manager sans noggin.

Luckily, after some heated discussion they decided to spare me and I was able to witness them try to reconcile the news that their once-great team could face imminent closure. It was a process, I noted, that was not dissimilar to the five stages of grief that followed a bereavement.

Denial.

Anger.

Bargaining.

Have a cigarette.

Acceptance.

Once they had all come to terms with the situation we quickly made a resolution that, rather than meekly accepting our fate, we would go on an aggressive marketing campaign to try and promote the Home Support Team to service users and their workers. But an early conversation with one of the people on my caseload (a potential customer) hinted at the difficulties that lay ahead:

"Ok," said Martin, after I'd finished going through it with him, "I've got money that I can spend on anything that makes me feel better?"

"That's right."

"So I could buy new trainers, go for a massage, do karate or…"

"Yes?"

"Or use it all to pay for that nurse to come round and nag me about taking the medication that makes me put on weight and dribble on my pillow?"

"Yes."

Jay-Z once told me that he could sell ice in the winter, fire in hell, he was a hustler, baby, who'll sell water to a well, but not even Jay-Z could persuade people to spend their personal budgets on the Home Support Team. We had come into health care to support people, not to try and sell them things. Besides, we were rubbish at it and it reminded me of when I was once asked to help sell tickets for a nightclub we had organised at university. Called Bubble, we had hired (at great cost) a huge bubble machine that was intended to give the venue an enchanted ambiance. Unfortunately the only thing it did was to coat the dancefloor in Fairy Liquid causing the four people we had managed to convince to buy a ticket to slip and slide around like newborn foals all night.

The Home Support Team clearly shared my ineptitude for marketing, yet we soldiered on, trying to deliver the best possible service to the (rapidly dwindling) people that used it.

One of these was Bruce, who smoked cigarettes in long black holders and had a propensity for spectacular acts of self-harm. It was not long after I had started working with the team that the office phone rang. I was the closest.

"Hello, Home Support Team," I answered brightly.

"Whe whe, whe whe," said the voice on the other end.

"Hello, Home Support Team," I repeated.

"Whe whe, whe whe."

"I'm sorry, could you repeat that please?"

"Whe whe, whe whe."

I pushed the receiver into my ear. "I didn't quite catch that."

"Whe whe, whe whe."

I turned to the team and gestured for them to quieten down. "That's better, now what was that again?"

"Whe whe, whe whe."

It was no use. I asked the team for complete silence.

"I'm really sorry but could you say that one more time?"

"I've cut, my throat."

The colour drained from me. It was Bruce; bleeding out whilst I'd had him on the phone for the last five minutes playing Chinese whispers.

Spencer, another person who used the Home Support Team, had obsessive compulsive disorder and had asked if a staff member could take him to the annual OCD conference. Keen to show that I was a hands-on manager and having nearly allowed one of the team's valued customers to choke on his own blood, I volunteered to do this. It was held in a large hotel in central London and comprised of speakers, question-and-answer sessions and a series of workshops. I had been unsure of what to expect but found it a warm, relaxed atmosphere. In fact, the only clue to it being an OCD conference was that when I went to the toilet there was a longer queue to wash your hands than to use the urinal.

I found the day informative and learned lots about the condition. For the last workshop of the day, Spencer had registered to attend a Body Dysmorphia session. Like OCD, Body Dysmorphia could be a crippling disorder in which people developed an obsessive preoccupation that some aspect of their appearance was flawed. This often led them to take exceptional measures to hide or fix it. Unlike OCD there was relatively little public understanding of it. At the workshop, sufferers were brought together, often for the first time, and were able to recount their experiences in a safe place. People told their stories of isolation, self-mutilation and suicide attempts. As one woman finished her traumatic account of placing her leg across a train track in the hope that the oncoming train would remove the limb, Spencer stood up. "I hate my knees when I wear swimming trunks," he announced to the silent audience who were still reeling from the horror of the train story.

For months, the Home Support Team struggled on, trying to promote a service to people who would much prefer to spend their personal budget on a mindfulness course and pony trekking. Inexplicably, higher management saw my desperate attempts at prolonging the life of the service as a beacon of good practice and asked me to go and talk to other teams about how they could make their service more viable. Unable to look my audience in the eye, I spoke about the importance of a positive mission statement, a clear promotional strategy and strong customer relations, whilst my team's caseload got smaller and smaller. I had not felt such a fraud since I had been pressed into doing a public lecture for my archaeology course. I had reluctantly agreed to do a talk on the archaeological evidence for suspicious deaths (so that I could call it Murder Most Trowel) and was asked if one of the cases I had described, in which a Viking woman had been found with twelve heavy stakes through her body, signified a suicide. This was a well-known practice performed by the rest of the community to prevent the soul of the person who had killed themselves leaving their body. Unfortunately, it was not well known to me and I spent the next twenty minutes trying to explain to the packed auditorium why I didn't think she had committed suicide as she would have struggled to get all of that wood into her.

Soon after returning from my motivational tour of other teams, I was called into my manager's office and was told that this highly reputable, long-established service that I had managed for less than six months would be closed and the staff would be merged into the Community Mental Health Team. My post as team leader would cease to exist and, having failed to save the team, I was naturally worried about my future.

Would I be unemployed?

Would I be moved to another service?

Would I have to return shamefaced to my old post?

Of course not; this was the NHS.

I got a promotion.

TWENTY-SIX

It had become clear to me soon (seconds) after accepting the post with the Home Support Team that this was not going to be a job for life and, whilst I tried to put all of my energy and enthusiasm into the team, I also kept an eye on the vacancy bulletin in case anything more stable became available.

A team leader post with a small Community Mental Health Team looked exciting but I struggled through the interview and was informed by the appointing officer that I had been unsuccessful. This was only the second time that I had failed to pass an interview; the first time had been many years earlier when I had applied to the Toys R Us management training programme. Not considering that they may have been interested in my ability to supervise staff, balance budgets and manage complaints, I spent the whole forty five minutes discussing Action Man's underpants, Optimus Prime's flimsy hinge and my idea for a range of Super Gran action figures. I even told them about my party piece of holding any Star Wars figure behind my back and, just by rubbing the head, being able to identify which one it was (though I occaisionally mistook Princess Leia Organa in Bespin Gown for Snaggletooth).

I didn't get the job (because of a general lack of management skills rather than my Snaggletooth blind spot).

*

A new team, the Early Intervention in Psychosis service, had recently been set up in our area. Targeting people who were experiencing hallucinations and delusions, it was based upon growing evidence that found that a period of intense support during the early stages of this illness achieved better long-term outcomes. The service tended to have more staff and lower caseloads than the less fashionable Community Mental Health Teams who hated them for it.

I met the current Early Intervention team leader on a Safeguarding Children course where she told me how enjoyable her job was. She also told me that she was due to leave the post soon as she was moving out of the area and that I should consider applying. For the rest of the day I could think of nothing else. Presentations on How to Recognise Abuse, Protocols for Raising Concerns and Supporting Others in Coping with Trauma passed me by. Workshops on Liaising with the Emergency Services and Identifying Potential Abusers were a blur. I got two out of twenty on the quiz at the end but by the time I was handed my certificate to say that I was a competent safeguarding practitioner my mind was set.

I would apply for the job.

Stung by my failure to get the Community Mental Health Team leader post, I prepared for this interview with a religious fervour.

I read everything relevant and anticipated every question:

What are your strengths?

I'm successful, effective and motivated.

What will you bring to this post?

Success, efficiency and motivation.

Why are you applying for this post?

Because the last team I managed was disbanded for being unsuccessful, ineffective and unmotivated.

There would be no Transformer talk this time, no reminiscing about Kung-Fu grips and Eagle Eyes. I was bloated with knowledge and, when the interview day finally arrived, I spewed it all over the interviewing panel.

After weeks of intense preparation things happened quickly.

On the evening after the interview Phil, the Early Intervention service manager, phoned to offer me the job. I accepted it immediately and agreed to start the following month. He suggested I meet the team before then and so I drove over to their offices the next day. Phil met me at the door and took me into the main part of the building which was swarming with doctors, support workers, nurses, psychologist, occupational therapists and other social workers.

"And which ones are in my team?" I asked.

"They're all in your team."

In all my preparation I hadn't given any thought to the size of the team I would be expected to manage.

There were twenty four employees in the Early Intervention in Psychosis team.

I'd barely coped with six in my last post.

Too far along now to back out, I went and handed in my notice to my old employers. I had worked in the building, with both the Community Mental Health Team and the

Home Support Team, for over ten years and, during that time, I had organised all manner of leaving do's.

For Dr Boleros I had presented a This is Your Life which culminated in him being presented with a hair brush covered in chocolate spread in recognition of the time he asked someone we were assessing if she was aware of any warning signs when she was becoming unwell.

"I tend to stick my brush up my husband's bottom," she replied nonchalantly.

For an Italian colleague who was leaving I hastily put together a vocal harmony group to sing an Italian medley that started with Quando, Quando, Quando and finished with Renee and Renata's spine-tingling Save Your Love My Darling.

And when a nurse with over forty years' service retired I organised a party that ended with me attempting to do the caterpillar off a table, my arms giving way and having a four inch carpet burn across my forehead for the next month.

How would they top that?

Two weeks before my last day my manager approached me.

"We thought we'd have a quiet drink after work for your leaving do."

"Sounds good," I said, wondering what she was really up to.

Quiet drink? Honestly!

A week before and I went into the secretaries' office.

"Are you all coming out this Friday?" I asked.

"I can't, I'm driving to my sisters."

"I'm out on a hen night."

"Sorry, but my babysitter's let me down."

"Ok," I said playing along.

Babysitter let me down. Right!

My last day finally arrived and at 5pm I went down to reception.

Three people waited for me.

"Shall we get going then?" said my manager putting her coat on. We walked across town to the pub in the park.

"You first," she said gesturing towards the door.

I opened the door with nervous excitement.

There was a loud cheer.

One of the regulars had won £3 on the quiz machine.

The other two people in the pub congratulated him as we went to the bar and ordered some drinks.

"To your new job," toasted my three colleagues, "cheers!"

As I drank I remembered this place had a large function room in the back.

I wonder?

An hour later I still wondered.

"I better be making a move," said my manager eventually, standing up and getting her coat. The others also had to go. After hugs and well wishes I made my way back to my flat.

As I got to my door I noticed a light was on.

I never left my light on.

Could it be?

My neighbour had a spare key and was friends with my manager.

I slowly opened the door.

I couldn't believe it.

I had left my light on.

TWENTY-SEVEN

For the first time in my career I was given my own office and so I promptly set about installing all of my reference books, journals, codes of practice and policy guides. I carefully put them in chronologic order to improve my speed of access and never opened any of them for the next two years.

During my interview I had outlined my plan to develop the service further and improve its already high standards. But as I had waffled on about performance objectives and outcome measures, I had not considered the sheer volume of complaints, crises and untoward incidents that I would be required to deal with each day. Though a senior colleague shared some of the supervision duties with me, it was hard to focus upon achieving 100% compliance with Department of Health standards when Julie, one of the team's nurses, had just used her black belt in jujitsu to take down a patient outside Woolworths.

Julie and I would hotly debate this incident in later supervisions and consider how other techniques, such as a calm voice and non-threatening body language, may be more effective than martial arts. Over time we were able to curb her bloodlust but every so often she would delight in dropping a bombshell on me that would turn my hair grey(er).

"Oh, and Cheryl told me that her dad strangled her three-year-old son a bit whilst they were playing Monopoly," she would casually mention at the end of our supervision.

Or…

"Well he's got rid of the rifle but he's still got the pistol and hunting knife."

Or…

"I've told her that she should snatch the kids from school at lunchtime and get on the first plane to Pakistan."

As a result of these passing comments I would then be required to spend hours on paperwork, phone calls and safeguarding meetings whilst Julie reminisced about the glory days where the throttling of a child would only require a brief note in the handover book.

Ying to Julie's yang was Alberto. Alberto was an experienced nurse, union representative and grand master of completing untoward incident forms. Anxious not to be held accountable for any disasters before he reached retirement (he was thirty-two) he would dash off a form at the drop of a hat, leaving me to investigate it in order to ascertain whether further safeguarding procedures were warranted. This was bearable when I was helping to keep babies safe and old people happy but when it was about drug-addled teenagers stubbing their toe in a supermarket it became an onerous task. On one occasion he handed me a three-page report detailing how one of his patients had been hurt whilst in the mosh pit of a death metal concert.

I was never quite sure if Alberto was serious about these forms or if it was a political statement but, since his breakdown at the team away day, I felt uncomfortable asking.

Soon after starting the job I had arranged an away day at a local village hall to review where we were as a team and where we wanted to go in the future (a venue with cleaner toilets). For the opening exercise I divided the team into small groups, provided each with a large blank canvas and a variety of arts and crafts materials and asked them to put something together that represented how they saw the service.

After half an hour, the first group were asked to feedback. They showed a lovely collage of sunshine, smiling people and positive slogans.

We all clapped and congratulated them.

Next was Alberto's group.

He marched to the front of the room and set his canvas down on the table.

"Lions led by donkeys," he announced, without further explanation.

The team studied it in silence.

I wasn't sure if I could fully appreciate the scope of the work but I could definitely pick out decapitated animal heads, people with their eyes whited out, offal and swear words scrawled in blood.

I found it difficult to know how to respond to this, primarily because I didn't want to come across as insensitive, but also because I was the only one who had taken up the challenge of coming in costume and was dressed head to toe as a Mexican.

"Thank you, Alberto," I said, nervously trying to untangle my moustache from my sombrero string, "shall we have the next group then?"

Just as I managed to solve one problem in the team another would quickly arise.

One member of staff told me that she had left her diary in Marks & Spencer's toilet whilst shopping for clothes on her lunch break. When she had gone back to retrieve it, it was nowhere to be found.

Luckily, on a recent Information Governance training session we had been told about the importance of removing any client identifiable information from diaries and I remembered this staff member actively agreeing with the importance of this.

"Did it have anything confidential in it?" I checked.

"Well, I'd used initials for the appointments."

"Excellent."

"But in the back I'd put a list of everyone's name and address and what medication they are on."

For those few minutes of M&S underwear shopping, I had to write to each person on her caseload (around thirty), explain what had happened and offer to meet with them to discuss it.

Eight of them took me up on the offer.

I hoped those knickers chafed.

Such breaches of confidentiality were regularly being reported in the media and I was anxious that my Pancake Day exploits remained my only foray into the newspapers. When the wife of Murray, one of our service users, contacted me to say that she had fled to her parents' home due to her husband's psychological abuse and under no circumstances should we disclose this to him, I took it very seriously. After discussing it with our medical records department it was agreed that I would put a high alert on his electronic records summarising the situation. This would then appear at the top of each document so that all staff, particularly his newly-qualified care coordinator Janet, were aware.

With this done I went back to the main tasks of team leadership; being told what to do by people above and being told to stick it in my pipe and smoke it by those below.

My priority at this time was to ensure that everyone who used the service had a copy of their care plan. Care plans were documents which summarised all of the support, treatment and interventions that had been put in place. For the geranium in our secretary's office, it would have included daily wiping of leaves, weekly watering, monthly mulch and annual repotting. For many of the people who used our service it consisted of take your medication and ring us if you're going to kill yourself (during office hours only).

With only days until an audit of our care plans was due to take place, I harassed team members to check that everyone on their caseload had a copy and, if not, to print one out and post it immediately.

I was at my desk the next day when a thought struck me. I rushed into the room next door.

"Janet? Have you given Murray a copy of his care plan?"

"No, but I sent one out to him. First class," she added proudly.

"And did you remove the bright red high alert off the top of the care plan that gave all the details of where and why his wife was hiding from him?"

Her eyebrows raised.

Her mouth opened.

She put her hand on her forehead.

"That would be a no then."

Later that day, my stomach in a knot, I had to phone his wife and explain that, despite her clear request, her husband now knew that she was staying with her parents.

I felt that, all things considered, she took it surprisingly well though she did ask for the name of our Chief Executive and I don't think it was to leave a compliment.

A large part of my role as team leader was to try and keep morale high and so, following these serious breaches of client confidentiality that some of the staff had made, I thought it would be a good idea for me to fuck up massively so that people wouldn't feel quite so bad about themselves.

Soon after the incident with Murray's wife, we started to work with another person who had recently fled an abusive relationship. During her initial assessment with one of our workers, she had disclosed that her alleged abuser was an NHS nurse and so this information was promptly hurled at me to deal with. Unsure of what to do, I spoke with our safeguarding lead who told me to immediately fax an ultra-confidential referral to the Disclosure and Barring Service. I found the form online and filled it in, detailing the name of the alleged abuser, their occupation, the hospital where they worked and the allegations against them. Having done this, I sent it to the office printer to be printed out ready for faxing.

I waited for a few moments but nothing happened.

I went and checked the printer. Online and full of paper.

I waited a bit longer.

Still nothing.

Seeing my growing agitation our secretary came over to help.

"It's been sent to another printer on the network," she said, clicking through the menus on my screen, "I hope it wasn't confidential."

The same Information Governance course that had told us not to record names in diaries had also warned us not to send confidential data over an unsecured network, citing a recent case in which a man's gender reassignment referral had come out of a printer at his local kebab house.

I had just sent allegations of systematic sexual abuse by a well-known healthcare worker to an unknown location.

"Of course it's not confidential," I assured her.

With sweating digits and a racing heart I punched in the number of our IT department. After negotiating thirty-six options and a twenty-minute wait, a toddler answered the phone.

I explained the situation to him, trying hard not to cry.

"Well," sighed the infant, "we use a network printing system in the Trust so your document could conceivably be anywhere in the county. You should really check the printer address before you send something."

I drew upon something I'd read in a book on mindfulness and imagined I was a raisin.

"Do you have the number of the printer it was sent to?" he asked.

Our secretary had scribbled it down for me and so I read it out.

"Ok," he said after a few minutes, "that is in the city hospital."

The city hospital where the alleged abuser worked.

Screeching into the hospital carpark, I threw the £18 needed for half an hour's parking into the machine and ran into the reception.

As I scanned the site map, unable to understand the layout of the departments, a hospital volunteer, clearly sensing the urgency of the situation, approached me.

"Are you after the toilet, my love?"

Eventually, after explaining I was incompetent rather than incontinent, I was directed to the corridor which was alleged to house the printer I sought and began a desperate search, aware that if someone else had got to the form before me I could be selling the Big Issue by tomorrow.

For each empty printer tray I found, a small part of me died.

The number of rooms I had left became less and less until only the office for Sexually Transmitted Diseases remained. Unlike the other forty-two printers I had found, this one had a pile of papers sitting in its out-tray. I grabbed them and looked at the top sheet.

Evidence based interventions for the treatment of aggressive genital warts.

My heart sank. I flicked through the rest.

Herpes in Teenagers.

Syphilis in Denmark.

Chlamydia in the 21st Century.

Finally, just as I was losing all hope, I found it, snuggled at the bottom. My form! With a huge sense of relief I scooped it up and drove triumphantly back to the office.

"I'm saved!" I told our secretary, triumphantly flinging it down on her desk.

Unfortunately, in my haste I'd grabbed the whole bundle of papers and Evidence based interventions for the treatment of aggressive genital warts was at the top.

"That's great," she said, taking a small step backwards.

TWENTY-EIGHT

I was only able to survive the early months of the job by working long hours and having a supportive manager. The two were to combine late one evening when, after coming back to the office to catch up on some notes, Phil, my manager, called.

"What are you up to?" he asked.

"Just a few things on my to-do list."

"It's 10.30!"

"I know, I won't be long, bye."

Two hours later he phoned back.

"Phil!" I said grabbing the receiver, "Ainsley's eyes moved!"

In the time since he had last phoned, I had taken some Neurofen Cold and Flu tablets which, when taken alongside my hayfever tablets, appeared to mimic the effects of a crack-cocaine speedball.

"What do you mean Ainsley's eyes moved?" he asked, concerned.

It was dark outside.

The wind was howling.

There was no one else in the building and Ainsley Harriot's photo on the side of a packet of his French Onion instant soup had just winked at me.

"He's watching me, Phil, he's fucking watching me!"

Phil sighed. "You need to go home now."

*

I would meet with Phil every month and talk through all the issues that had come up in the weeks before. The outcome of these discussions would be scribbled down during our meeting and handed to our team secretary to type them up formally.

Around this time, I developed a severe case of paediphobia; a fear of children, specifically, in my case, a fear that I would have more. There were a range of treatments available which varied in severity, from the withdrawal method (which was responsible for my first child) to abstinence (which was responsible for my first divorce). In the end I plumped for the nuclear option: a vasectomy. When I'd discussed it with people who had gone through the procedure, I was reassured that it was reasonably painless. Indeed, minutes before my operation, the post-op men recuperating in their y-shaped chairs with their legs akimbo told me the same. But, as I lay on the operating slab in exotic pain, smelling burning tubes and being told by a bored agency nurse to look at the maze puzzle on the ceiling, I knew I had been duped.

I staggered out into the waiting room and eased myself into my own y-shaped chair.

"That was horrible," I whimpered.

"We know," said the others and we all burst out crying.

This was relevant to my supervision with Phil because I would have to take time off work to have the operation and, not keen for our team secretary (who already thought I had aggressive genital warts) to know the precise reason for my leave, I asked him if he could not record it on my notes.

"No problem," he assured me, "I'll just put something vague in."

The next day the secretary handed me the typed-up notes. I read them through. At the top of page one it said David will be having some time off due to medical reasons (haemorrhoids).

Phil gave me a great deal of freedom in my job and nowhere did I exercise this more than in staff interviews. At a recruitment training day I had recently attended I asked whether there were any limits to the type of questions we were allowed to ask the interviewee. After discussion it was generally agreed that, as long as it wasn't offensive and all applicants were asked the same questions, we could be as creative as we liked. This was music to my ears as I had had a longstanding cynicism about the effectiveness of standard interview questions finding the best candidates.

How do you manage stress? How do you deal with conflict? How do you work in a team?

They could all be easily anticipated and prepared for, often reflecting how many interviews the applicant had been through rather than any sense of their character.

This had been highlighted years earlier when, on an interview panel, I scored someone full marks and was ready to recommend that they were offered the post when I saw them get very ratty with Edith, who was merely interrogating them about their sexual persuasions. There was often a disparity, it appeared, between a person's performance in an interview and their warmth and empathy in the workplace.

When one of our team went on maternity leave I was told we could interview for her vacant post and this gave me the perfect opportunity to apply my theory to practice.

After thanking the applicants for coming and giving them an overview of the job I asked my opening question.

"In view of the pressures on local authority funding, the impact that this has had upon service delivery and the need for more focussed, cost effective interventions, could you tell me, if you were a ready-meal, which one you would be and why?"

Whilst other members of the panel were uncomfortable with this approach and felt terrible at the interviewees' discomfort, I maintained that it was an effective technique for getting a measure of a person.

Viv, the successful applicant (vegetarian spaghetti Bolognese), turned out to be a valuable asset to the team.

And such questions weren't solely limited to finding the best candidate.

One man, who we were later interviewing for a vacant nurse post, was scoring highly on my colleagues' strengths and weaknesses questions. But when I asked, with the move towards the recovery model and greater levels of service user participation, which jungle animal he would be and why, he became unhinged.

"I'd be an elephant," he spat, "the true king of the jungle. They're quiet but can stomp all over anyone that gets in their way! Trample them flat. Stop for no one."

We thanked him for attending the job and promptly offered the job to a South American squirrel monkey (highly creative and works well in a team).

TWENTY-NINE

O ver time I became used to the daily responsibilities of a team leader but I knew in my heart that it wasn't for me. Whilst I loved the sense of autonomy it provided, I hated the daily conflicts that were intrinsic to the role and would lie awake at night replaying those that had happened and worry about those which were to come. Allocating complex cases to people who didn't want them, arguing with other teams about who should be doing what and addressing why a staff member was always off when it was a full moon did not come naturally to me and I would get a knot in my stomach when I had to face them. The general feeling seemed to be that I was doing well but I constantly questioned whether I was cut out for all of the nitty gritty aspects that came with the job. Give me the task of ensuring that we were up-to-date with relevant policies and I was fine (everyone had to present one in a randomly selected musical style leading to our psychologist rapping the Infection Control Policy over an instrumental of Ice Ice Baby – "Alright stop, wash your hands and listen.") But having to discipline a member of staff for repeatedly falling asleep during assessments ("I just feel that no one listens to me," sobbed the patient before looking up to see our nurse sleeping with her mouth open) was just too much.

On the rare occasions when I was able to undertake

direct work with people who used the Early Intervention Service I felt on safer ground but even this could prove troublesome.

Margot was a civil servant who, in recent years, had become convinced that she was under constant surveillance by an unknown enemy. She had stopped going into work, got rid of most of the electrical equipment in her house and was convinced that the only place that she would be safe was Geneva. The nurse who worked with her had tried everything to help, but since Margot had started to think her food and drink had been tampered with and reduced them accordingly, things had reached a crisis point.

After much discussion it was agreed that I would coordinate a Mental Health Act assessment and, after interviewing Margot in her home, the doctors and I concluded that compulsory hospital admission was the only option for her to receive the treatment she needed.

We explained our decision and the reasoning behind it.

Margot said she was not going.

The doctors duly left and I called for an ambulance to transport her to hospital and the police to encourage her to be transported.

I then waited outside in my car.

Experience had taught me that once the assessment had been completed and a decision to admit a person had been made, no good came from spending the next few hours in their home waiting for the ambulance to arrive. This was not because of risk, discomfort or any feelings of guilt but rather, the tendency for people, once the pink papers had been signed, to make an immediate and full recovery. Those men and women who had been manic/suicidal/thought-disordered/mute during the assessment would suddenly become calm/positive/clear-thinking/talkative once everyone else had gone. And with the application completed, the doctor's recommendations signed and the hospital bed booked, it was almost impossible to bring the process to a halt once it had begun.

One young man, who had been so floridly psychotic prior to the decision to detain him that he had thought I was one of the Bee Gees, proceeded to give me a detailed overview of the political gains made by the feminist movement whilst I waited for the police to arrive to take him to a locked ward. Another elderly woman, who I had arranged secure transport for after she had sunk her choppers into an unsuspecting doctor's hand, ended up giving them directions to the hospital that would shave ten minutes off their journey time.

And so I decided that I would wait in my car outside Margot's house.

The ambulance control centre always gave an estimated time of two hours before a crew would attend the scene. In all the years that I have been an Approved Social Worker they have only met this deadline once. On all the other occasions, I would wait for hours and hours without so much as a whiff of a paramedic. People being conveyed under the Mental Health Act were not classed as an emergency and would be bumped down the priority list if something more urgent came in (heart attack, stroke, dinky wounded by oral sex). Several times I would be warmly welcoming an ambulance after I had waited for most of the day, only for it to suddenly screech off in front of me with blue lights flashing. Add to this the difficulties of trying to synchronise the arrival of the police with the ambulance, and things became near impossible.

"Phone us when the ambulance is there," police control would instruct me, "and then we'll come."

"Phone us when the police are there," ambulance control would instruct me, "and then we'll come."

"The ambulance is here now," I would fib to police control.

"The police are here now," I would fib to ambulance control.

I would then nervously wait for whoever came first so that I could explain to them that I was, in fact, a fibber.

Once I had made the calls for the police and ambulance to take Margot to hospital there was nothing left to do but wait.

And wait.

The sun beat down on my car, heating the vinyl inside and turning the multiple bird shits on the outside to concrete. In my excitement to show my team what a competent, confident practitioner I was, I had rushed out with no provisions; no water, no banana. I knew that there was a convenience store around the corner but I also knew that if I was to leave there was a real risk that Margot would abscond. I didn't want to take this chance and so I sat and braised in my own sweat.

Two hours later and there was still no sign of the emergency services. My throat was parched and my tummy rumbled. I had repeatedly searched my car in the hope of finding anything that would sustain me. All I had managed to find was a dried-up, tasteless fruit gum (that, after forty minutes, I realised was a button) and a wet wipe that I desperately dabbed over my cracked lips.

Another hour passed and still I waited.

I would occasionally catch a glimpse of Margot moving

behind her net curtains but, other than that, there was nothing as the hours rolled on and the temperature rose.

I was just preparing to swig down the fluid that my disposable contact lenses came in when I heard a sound in the distance.

Bells on the wind.

I strained to pick them out.

There was a familiarity to them.

Something comforting.

And then it became clear.

A glockenspiel rendition of The Sun Has Got His Hat On.

Finally, I thought, the madness has consumed me.

I greeted it with open arms.

But then, in my rear-view mirror, I saw the source of the sound: Ginaro's Ice Cream Van, covered with badly painted pictures of ice lollies, screwballs and Hong Kong Phooey.

I tentatively looked over at Margot's net curtains and back to the ice cream van.

It was so close.

I could be waiting here for hours more.

Without further hesitation, I jumped out of the car and ran to the van. When I returned, minutes later, with two Mini Milks and a Nobbly Bobbly, the house remained quiet.

I was still trying to lick some stray Bobblies from around my mouth when the ambulance and, mercifully, the police, arrived. Although I was sure Margot would not come without a police presence, I was keen to initially try with just the paramedics.

We went to the door and worryingly, found it ajar.

I pushed it open and called in.

No response.

We went in to her front room where earlier in the day she had told me her Magimix was listening to us. The police joined us and we looked through the house. There were clothes on the floor, food on the table, but no Margot.

She was gone.

She must have legged it when I was deciding whether to buy Mini Milks or a Strawberry Mivvi.

I knew that there was nothing left to do now but to secure the house and leave. I watched as the ambulance and police van, which I had waited five hours for, leave. As I packed up my papers I found an old mobile number of Margot's which the GP had provided me with. I sent her a text asking where she was, although I knew in my heart that with her suspicion of electronics and fear of hospital admission she was not going to respond.

My phone stayed silent.

Four days later I received a text back.

Geneva.

Since Margot was technically detained under the Mental Health Act when she fled the country, I had to notify our formidable Mental Health Act administrator who gave me a severe lecture about leaving her alone in her home, even if it was for an emergency toilet break (I thought better of telling her about the ice cream van). Because all of the paperwork had been signed before she ran, the Trust was now required to keep a bed available for the next three months on the off-chance that Margot got bored of wandering around the Alps eating cheese fondue and came home.

She didn't.

It would be the same formidable Mental Health Act administrator that I had to see after the admission of Derick (he of the knife in hand and fountain of blood pumping from his radial artery) to submit his section papers.

Part of the administrator's role was to scrutinise the documents and ensure that they were correctly completed. She did this with gusto, and was a stickler for detail, previously giving me grief for scribbled dates, scrawled signatures and slapdash addresses.

"I hope they're all in order," she said, peering over her spectacles, red pen at the ready.

With hands cupped and buttocks clenched, I slowly approached her desk and poured Derick's section paper confetti into a small pink mound in front of her.

THIRTY

Reluctant to accept that the job of team leader was too much for me, I could only see two ways out; I could be fired for gross incompetence or leave in a body bag. So, when my wife told me of her wish for a move to the countryside, I was ecstatic.

"It would mean that I would have to give up my job," I said ruefully, "but, if it's what you really want, then I'll do it. For you."

I handed my notice in the next day and skipped out of the building.

I phoned my wife.

"It's done," I said sorrowfully.

She was very excited and very grateful but worried about what I'd had to sacrifice.

"Well, I know it's what you want, my dear," I reassured her half-heartedly, thinking how I would never have to investigate another pointless safeguarding concern or discipline Julie for using her one-inch death punch at the day centre.

To mark my departure, one of the team suggested that we all go to a stately home that held regular themed nights. After my last surprise leaving do (the surprise being that no one came), I was grateful for anything and so I readily agreed to go to their next event, A Night of Hollywood Glamour.

Though it has been oft-disputed by my colleagues, I continue to maintain that on the front of the flyer that advertised A Night of Hollywood Glamour was a picture of Frank Sinatra and Chewbacca. This image, real or otherwise, heavily influenced my choice of outfit for the night.

The first sign that something was amiss was when several of the nurses that I worked with arrived at my house to give me a lift to the venue. They were dressed in long flowing dresses with elaborate hairstyles.

The receptionist at the stately home was my second clue.

"You're lucky I'm going to let you in," she told me curtly.

Final confirmation of my inappropriate dress came when I walked into the packed hall and two hundred-plus heads turned to me.

"Skyfall," crooned the cabaret singer into her microphone, "Skyfall, Sky...Why the fuck is he dressed as an Oompa Loompa?"

By now my bright orange makeup was dripping onto my white dungarees and my green wig was sagging.

I desperately looked around for Chewbacca.

We moved to the countryside because it had low rates of rainfall and high rates of mental disorder, and chose to live in a quiet, rural hamlet that the estate agent described as idyllic.

A colleague called it the village of the damned.

Our house was a small thatched cottage with many traditional features including crumbling plaster, rising damp and a ghost. The previous occupiers had employed a local cleaner and we decided to give her a try, though it soon became clear that it was not going to work as I found having a cleaner too awkward, particularly one who was rubbish at cleaning. She told me that she had a connection to the spiritual world and was in regular communication with the soul of a young orphan boy that wandered our bedrooms.

"Then could you ask him to give you a hand dusting the pelmets?" I asked and we never saw her again.

My wife was first to find a job and quickly adapted to the nuances of rural medicine (mobile clinics, telephone consultations, leeches). Social worker posts were scarcer but I eventually saw an advert for a post in another Early Intervention in Psychosis service and phoned the manager.

"Would I have any opportunity to supervise other staff?" I asked.

"No."

"Would I be able to take a lead on safeguarding?"

"No."

"Would I be able to contribute to the development of the service provision?"

"No."

"Perfect," I said and promptly applied.

I had one day off between ending my previous job and starting my new one. I had not had a chance to unpack and so I arrived late for my first team meeting, wearing my wedding shirt, pea green tracksuit bottoms and flip flops. I was introduced to my new colleagues, given a list of people I would be working with and got going.

The first thing I did was to go and visit the local hospital as, not only had I found it helpful to have good links with the ward, but my manager had asked me to try and raise the profile of our team.

I went to reception and explained that I would like to have a look around.

"And who are you?" asked the receptionist curtly.

"I'm from the Care Quality Commission," I decided to tell him.

The Care Quality Commission is the statutory regulating body that monitors the health sector. It has many powers including the power to shut a service down. What I wasn't aware of, as I watched the colour drain from the receptionist's flabby face, was that an unannounced Care Quality Commission inspection had taken place weeks earlier with devastating results. The hospital had been classed as failing, a final warning had been issued, staff changes had been imposed and a comprehensive set of targets had been set which needed to be met to ensure the hospital's continued operation. A further unannounced visit was due to take place to see if all of this had been carried out.

"Yes sir," said the receptionist, springing up, "take a seat sir, I'll be right back sir."

And with that he rushed upstairs to summon higher management.

As I stood alone, waiting for them to descend upon me, I considered making a run for it but knew that my flip flops would only take me so far. Instead, I decided that I would stay and face the music – which I did and, by the time they allowed me to leave, I felt confident that I had succeeded in raising the profile of our team.

My attempts to forge good relationships with the services I hoped to spend a significant part of my career working alongside had got off to a bad start and so I hoped that the next day's visit to the local Community Mental Health Team would be more positive.

It wasn't.

I have learned over time that the most important person in the team is usually the receptionist and so, on arrival at the Community Mental Health Team offices, I set about building a positive relationship with her. Things went well and, as there was a staff lunch taking place for a colleague who was leaving, she asked if I would cover her for twenty minutes so that she could attend.

"No problem," I said.

I had frequently helped out on reception in my previous jobs and had always enjoyed it.

After ten minutes a woman came to the desk.

"Could I see someone from duty please?"

"Of course," I said, giving her my warmest smile.

I found the speed dial for duty and called it. The line was engaged.

"Take a seat and I'll try them again soon."

I sat and read through one of the induction packs I had been given.

Five minutes later I tried duty again but the line remained busy.

"I'll give it another few minutes," I called across the waiting room to her.

A few minutes passed and I tried again. Still engaged.

"Can I ask why you're here? I asked as I put down the receiver.

"I've taken an overdose."

I nearly fell off my chair.

I ran and told the manager who immediately called for an ambulance which blue-lighted her to hospital to have her stomach pumped.

My final indiscretion of this first week in my new job came on the way to a home visit in a remote village. It had been pouring with rain for the whole week and, as I wound my way through tight country lanes, I was brought to a sudden halt by a flooded dip in the road.

A tractor coming the other way was slowly negotiating the three feet of water and pulled up next to me when it was safely through.

The farmer came over.

"She's a deep one!" he said (everything had a gender in the countryside).

"Is this the worst of it?" I asked.

"Well, he [road] clears up soon but don't be taking her [car] in or she'll [water] flood her [car] right up and you'll need him [tractor] to pull her [car again] out."

I thanked him for the advice, waited until I was sure he was out of sight and then ploughed into the dip.

It was when my footmat started to float that I knew I had made a mistake. Too deep to turn back and taking on too much water to stop, I pushed onwards, my car juddering, the engine whining. Just as the rising tide started to kiss the turn-up of my trousers and I was mentally preparing myself for a watery grave, I struck dry land. After offering up thanks to Poseidon, Neptune and Captain Birdseye, I bailed out my shoes, wrung out my socks and continued my voyage towards the village.

When I eventually arrived, I was suddenly overcome by a terrible stench. The water in my footwell had drained away and left a sewage residue in its wake. I whacked the fans on full, unaware that parts of the engine were still flooded with pond water, causing the car to be instantly filled with a thick fog. Panicking that it was smoke and about to blow, I pulled onto the pavement and dived out of the car.

As steam billowed through my open door and I lay dazed on the ground, I became aware of a continuous, high-pitched sound.

Was it an acquired brain injury I had sustained?

Tinnitus?

My death rattle?

No, it was an elderly lady on her mobility scooter holding down her horn.

"You there," she called, pointing at my car which was blocking the pavement, "move her!"

THIRTY-ONE

Once I had negotiated the challenging first week, things got easier and I soon found myself driving around the county looking at breathtaking scenery, listening to soothing birdsong and smelling the liquid chicken shit that they regularly dumped over the crops. On my travels I would meet with lots of interesting characters, try to get to the bottom of what was going on for them and look at what the most appropriate support might be to help in their recovery.

After a while it became clear that a major part of my work would be to try and differentiate whether people's problems were as a result of mental illness or just being born in the countryside.

The differences between the two were subtle but over time I learned to identify them. One was characterised by social withdrawal, communication difficulties, a lack of energy, blunted affect and disordered thoughts.

The other was mental illness.

The people on my caseload were widely dispersed in remote villages and I would often drive for hours only to find that they were not at home, fast asleep or too engrossed in Grand Theft Auto to walk the two metres to their front door. In previous jobs I had always enjoyed missed appointments as it gave me time to relax and catch up on notes but in the country it usually meant an additional two hours stuck behind a tractor, being peppered with manure whilst the driver phoned his farmer friends and made roll-ups between his knees.

Leo was one of the first people I worked with in my new job and I met him just as he was starting to become unwell. I had gone to see him at school after concerns had been raised by family members about a sudden change in his character and, on spending some time with him, I was also worried that something was wrong. He was vague, distant and confused. I called the child psychiatrist who agreed to see him but would need him to attend her clinic in another part of the county.

"I'll drive him over," I said confidently.

The journey started well but, as we hurtled along the main road followed closely by a line of heavy goods vehicles, Leo turned to me anxiously.

"Where are you taking me?" he asked.

"To see a doctor," I reminded him, having already gone through the plan in full.

Without warning he reached for the door handle and pulled it. The door swung open. I grabbed onto him as he tried to jump out. We were doing 50mph on a single lane with a twenty-ton articulated lorry several metres behind us.

"Let me go!" he shouted, as he tried to wriggle free.

I had no idea what to do. I desperately looked for somewhere to pull in but there was nothing. The force of the wind pushed the door closed but Leo tried to open it again. I wrestled him back with my left arm, trying to keep the car steady with my right. My shoulder went into spasm and I knew that I wasn't going to be able to keep holding him back for much longer.

As we struggled, a new song came on the radio and, as dramatically as he had started, Leo suddenly stopped.

"I love this song," he said excitedly and turned it up.

Minutes later we arrived at the hospital, me in a state of deep shock and Leo singing along to The Return of the Mack.

With time, space and copious amounts of antipsychotic medication Leo eventually recovered and decided that he wanted to spend the summer holidays with his extended family in Southern Europe. Never one for moderation, he intended to travel for three days on a coach from London before staying in rural Spain for eight weeks. Fearful of a relapse, I hastily had a letter translated into Spanish so that people would know what to do if he became unwell (neutralise with Mark Morrison and take to hospital). In preparation for this epic journey, Leo packed a vast suitcase containing all of his clothes, toiletries and medication. He also took his guitar.

I later found out that on arrival at the coach station, the driver had insisted that Leo could only take one piece of luggage: his battered acoustic guitar or his suitcase filled with all of his worldly possessions.

Naturally Leo chose the guitar.

With no clothes, toiletries or medication, he somehow managed to survive the trip and came back, several months later, tanned and well. Most remarkable was the fact that, on having been told that he needed to leave his suitcase, he had shoved it behind a bus shelter in Kings Cross and, despite it being left in central London during a time of high terrorist alert, he was able to retrieve it on his return.

His mum, Leo told me, had been very impressed that he had managed to wash and fold all of his clothes prior to arriving home.

I met Henrietta after she had gone into a church to ask for an exorcism and the vicar had given her the details of the local mental health team. Henrietta experienced a wide range of symptoms which were ever-changing in severity and nature and I, along with four psychiatrists, two psychologists, a colour therapist and a medium, struggled to understand their cause. The task was made more difficult by Henrietta's insistence on throwing herself into therapy after therapy in the hope of finding rapid relief from her distress. In the three months that I'd known her she had already dipped her toe into Accelerated Experiential Dynamic Psychotherapy, Dialectical Behaviour Activation and Classical Adlerian Postural Integration, all with little effect.

On one visit she told me that she wanted to try Holotropic Breathwork which was, according to Henrietta, an approach being successfully pioneered across Scandinavian mental health services. Like many of the other interventions she had researched, I had never heard of Holotropic Breathwork and brought the conversation back to my areas of expertise; housing, benefits and evidence based interventions for the treatment of aggressive genital warts.

The following week I met with Henrietta's parents to complete a carer's assessment. In recognition of the tremendous strain that carers experience, there was a legal obligation to offer an assessment to anyone who had been identified as a carer.

I hated doing them.

Led by a prescriptive questionnaire, the assessment would begin by getting the exhausted carer to detail the huge amounts of emotional and practical help they had to provide, free of charge, on a daily (and nightly) basis. We would then look at the toll that this was taking on their physical and mental health, their quality of life and their other relationships, before moving on to consider what types of help may be of benefit to them. This could include financial support, adaptations in the home, medical help and access to counselling. With this list compiled I would then have to tell them that the only help I was able to access was a telephone helpline that frequently went unanswered and a carers group run by Barbara who spent the majority of the meeting complaining about her angina.

And so, with a heavy heart, I arrived at Henrietta's parents' home.

"Come in," they said, taking me into their front room, "have a seat."

I sat down and took a deep breath, already feeling on the back foot. Not only had I forgotten the questionnaire and was trying to look competent by writing on the only piece of paper I could find in my car (a receipt from Argos) but they had also insisted that I took off my shoes which revealed five elaborately varnished toes (courtesy of my six-year-old daughter) poking through a large hole in my sock.

"She wants to go to Switzerland," they announced.

What they didn't mention was that for the last five days Henrietta had become obsessed with getting on a plane to Dignitas where she would pay to have herself euthanized.

I thought they were talking about her wanting to access Holotropic Breathwork.

"Well, if that's what she wants," I said, "it might be for the best."

They looked aghast.

"But..." stammered his dad.

"It's just a shame that it's not available on the NHS," I continued, "it sounds ideal for someone like Henrietta. Now, could you tell me your dates of birth please?"

Her mum started to sob quietly.

THIRTY-TWO

Charles stood out because he wore a monocle and the front page of his electronic notes recorded his status as informally dead. He wasn't dead, but had little going on his life and so I took him to visit a farm project in the hope of getting him engaged in some voluntary work. The owner, who had recently been awarded an O.B.E. for her tireless endeavour, spent the whole morning showing him around the facilities and introducing him to the staff. At the end of the tour we all gathered together for a beautiful lunch created entirely from organic produce grown on the farm.

"So, Charles," the owner loudly asked as the meal came to an end, "what do you think of our little set up then?"

The rest of the room quietened down and turned to us expectantly.

"I think you all need to put down the doobies and do some proper work," he replied as I tried to disappear into my nasturtium risotto.

One morning I received a message asking me to call a father who was very worried about his daughter. He had left his number and so I phoned immediately. He explained, in whispered tones, that he thought his daughter's mental health was deteriorating. He was desperate for her to get help but she had refused all offers. He wanted me to do something but didn't want her to know that he had contacted services as this might damage their relationship. I racked my brain for a way in but, without being able to disclose her dad's concerns, it was tricky. Eventually I decided that I would pay her an unannounced visit.

As I rang the doorbell it occurred to me that I should have spent more time planning what I would say if she opened the door. I hadn't bothered to do this because I was confident that she wouldn't open the door.

She opened the door.

"Oh hello," I said, taken aback, "I... urm...I work for mental health services and thought I would just...pop in..."

She looked pointedly at a sign on the door that listed a wide range of occupations and character types that weren't welcome to just pop in. I couldn't see duplicitous social worker on there and so I carried on.

"I thought I would just pop in and...introduce myself... and tell you what I do."

I braced myself for the door to be slammed. It wasn't. Despite the randomness of my visit, she invited me in and, over the next hour, told me about what was happening to her. I listened and arranged to come back the following week.

And the week after that.

Over time I was delicately able to introduce the idea of stopping cannabis (which she did), starting medication (which she did) and coming to our social group (which she did) and as a result her mental health dramatically improved.

Several months later I received a message asking me to call her. She had left her number and so I phoned immediately. She explained, in whispered tones, that she thought her dad's mental health was deteriorating. She was desperate for him to get help but he had refused all offers. She wanted me to do something but didn't want him to know that he had contacted services as this might damage their relationship.

"I'll try my best," I assured her, "I've faced a similar situation before."

One of the first pieces of work that I would complete with people was to look at their Early Warning Signs. This involved identifying the subtle changes that might occur when they were becoming unwell and considering what action they could take to prevent it from happening again. Common warning signs include poor sleep, irritability and a change in appetite. For Adam it was making salt pentagrams in the kitchen, knocking through the ceiling with a sledgehammer and driving around England in a stolen car, looking for a witch doctor to remove an ancient voodoo curse that the man in Morrisons had placed upon him.

On the risk assessment form we were required to complete for each person we worked with, Adam ticked nearly every box.

Harm to self, harm to others, harm from others, risk of accidents, risk of damage to property, unsafe use of medication, unsafe use of drugs, unsafe use of alcohol and impulsive behaviour.

The only box that remained blank was possession of weapons and this finally got a tick on the day I helped him move out of the flat he'd been evicted from. As he loaded his computer games and clothes into carrier bags, he casually reached up into the chimney flume and pulled out a loaded crossbow.

"Jesus Christ, Adam!" I exclaimed as he tried to pass it to me, "you can't have that!"

"Don't worry," he said reassuringly, "it's not very accurate."

The Early Intervention in Psychosis Service is commissioned to work with people for three years, following which service users are either transferred to the Community Mental Health Team or discharged back to their GP. Wherever possible we aim for the latter but with Adam the risks were too high and his mental health too unstable to allow this.

Months after his transfer to the team, I was out walking with his new care coordinator from the Community Mental Health Team when I asked her how Adam was doing.

"I have no idea," she told me.

Adam hadn't been seen since the day of his transfer. He had missed appointments with his doctor and meetings with his nurse who had been unable to do home visits due to Adam's lack of a home. As we speculated as to what fate may have befallen him, a muffled cry came from a nearby building site. We both turned to see a man in a welding mask waving an industrial angle grinder at us. He put it down and came over. As he got closer he took off the mask and, to our horror, we saw that it was Adam.

"Keep this to yourself," he whispered, "I don't want the social finding out."

Some time after this a colleague told me that she and her fiancé had put down a deposit on a new build flat; the first ever home they would own together. She described where it was and it soon became clear that it was the building Adam had been working on. I didn't have the heart to tell her that Adam, a man who was assessed as posing a high risk of damage to property, had been involved in its construction.

THIRTY-THREE

Though I had been Luke's social worker for over three years, I had only managed to see him on just two occasions. And so, when I received a tipoff from the police to say that he had been spotted in a neighbouring county, I quickly packed my panic alarm and set off to find him.

Due to the potential risks of trying to engage with someone who strongly wished to disengage, my manager insisted that I did not go alone and so I arranged for a worker from the local mental health team to meet me there.

There was a field in which a local woman walking her Labradoodle had recently seen a young man behaving erratically and so, after joining up with my colleague from the community team, we began our search.

An early morning fog covered the field and a wolf (or possibly a Labradoodle) howled menacingly in the distance. I clung to my NHS issue panic alarm aware that, with the feeble whistle it emitted, it would be of more use to throw it at a potential attacker than set it off. After half an hour of scouring the area we were about to give up when we stumbled upon it; a ramshackle barn concealed amongst the undergrowth.

"There it is," I gulped, "shall we see if he's in?"

We walked towards it together, neither of us wanting to reach it first. Tiptoeing through empty tins of paint, broken vinyl records and the occasional demonic doll's head, we eventually got to the door.

"I'm going to knock," I whispered.

I tapped on the door, ready to leg it at the first sign of peril.

There was nothing.

"Open it," suggested my colleague, from far behind me.

I pushed it open and we slowly went inside. There was a shopping trolley on its side and rubbish on the floor but little else. Like a Native American tracker, I crouched down and picked up a discarded carrier bag. Inside there was a sandwich packet which I carefully turned in my hands. I examined the splash of dried mayonnaise on the inside lid; touched it to measure its consistency, sniffed it to understand its stench. I rubbed some cheese between my fingers and held up a piece of wilted lettuce to the light.

"Its two days old," I said.

"How can you know that?" asked my impressed colleague.

"There's a receipt with it."

Luke was back.

I was allocated to work with Luke following his admission to a local secure psychiatric hospital under the Mental Health Act. He had been picked up by police in London after he had spent three hours standing in Sainsburys' freezer aisle with a bag of hair and a knife. Luckily the hair turned out to be his own and the knife a flick-comb. Police were sufficiently concerned, however, to take him to a nearby A&E where he was assessed and swiftly transferred to a facility in our catchment area.

My first job with Luke was to escort him to a less secure

unit where he could begin to prepare for a return to the community. Overnight leave was approved and I gave him a lift, stopping briefly at a petrol station for fuel and snacks. As I queued, Luke and I chose a bar of chocolate each. I reached the front of the queue and, as I started to pay, Luke asked if he could change his mind and swap his Curly Wurly for something else. I agreed and waited whilst the line of people behind me grew. After a few minutes Luke returned with a shopping basket full of cereal, bananas and a fruit loaf.

"Is this ok?" he asked, putting the basket in front of the cashier.

Pressured by the grumblings coming from behind, I hurriedly paid for it all and we finished our journey to the unit. After helping Luke settle in we agreed that I would return the next day.

When I arrived the following morning the staff told me that he had absconded five minutes after I had left and spent the night missing, sustained, no doubt, by cereal, bananas and a fruit loaf.

In the following years my main task was to coordinate searches for him, desperate to find him before he became unwell again. I became consumed with this task and would imagine I saw Luke everywhere; in the supermarket, at the leisure centre, standing in the background of the Antiques Roadshow whilst someone was having their duelling pistols valued.

But it was inevitably the police, not me, that found him.

The next time he came to the attention of services he was immediately admitted back to the local secure psychiatric hospital. I received a message to say he was there and drove over as fast as I could.

By the time I arrived he had escaped.

A staff debriefing was held to examine how someone was able to leave the hospital so quickly and so easily. The ward manager sombrely read out the clinical note that had been written by a student nurse, minutes before Luke had done one:

"Luke appears bright and full of spirits this morning. I observed him in the communal kitchen interacting with other patients and putting four boxes of cereal and a bunch of bananas into his satchel."

The next time I saw him he was in prison, having been arrested for the serious offence of threatening a police officer with a vase. He was awaiting trial at which, his solicitor later informed me, he was asked whether he pleaded guilty or not guilty.

Dressed in paisley trousers, a flowery shirt and a tartan waistcoat, he had replied, "Just chillaxing, m'lord," and was promptly placed on remand.

After travelling three hours to see him in prison, he refused to meet with me and was subsequently transferred back to hospital.

Throughout this time, I had been meeting with Luke's dad who was naturally worried about whether his son was safe or not. At the outset of his prison stay, Luke had been clear that he did not want him to know where he was and he was judged to have the capacity to make this decision. I raised this with our lead confidentiality officer who confirmed that we had a legal obligation to uphold Luke's wish not to inform his dad of his current circumstances. This put me in a very difficult situation as I was scheduled to meet with him the following week. I asked my manager what she thought I should do.

"Couldn't you tell him that you don't know where Luke is, but indicate with facial gestures that he's safe?" she suggested.

The thought of this poor man not only having to deal with the strain of a missing son but also a social worker appearing to have some form of palsy attack was too much. I resolved to find another way around the problem.

A solution soon presented itself when, days after we had visited Luke's ramshackle barn (which he called his chalet retreat), he was readmitted back into hospital and detained under the Mental Health Act. As his dad was his Nearest Relative there was now a legal obligation to tell him about his circumstances which I did, immediately. A review meeting was hastily organised by the hospital and I was invited to attend. I gave the gathered professionals a brief overview of Luke's history before he was invited in to join us. He had now been with the Early Intervention Team for three years and, although this was only the second time I had met him face-to-face, my involvement would now come to an end and a new worker would be allocated from his local team. I hoped that in this time Luke had developed some insight into his situation and would accept the support he needed at this stage in his life. As I listened to him assure the doctor that he would stay in hospital, comply with treatment and not try to abscond, I felt optimistic, though this was tempered slightly when a healthcare professional came into the room to report that she had just discovered a bundle of knotted sheets under his bed which he planned to scale the fence with.

THIRTY-FOUR

When I moved out to the country I was prepared for the slow pace of life, the vast expanses of rolling fields, the abundance of poor quality tattoos and the mild undercurrent of racism. What I hadn't expected was an availability of illegal drugs that made the crack-infested streets of West Baltimore, USA look like the Hundred Acre woods. Marijuana, cocaine, heroin, ecstasy, amphetamines, ketamine, acid; all seemed freely available in an area where I had thought that the most potent substance on offer would be homemade pickle.

Terry was someone who embraced this culture and presented me with a conundrum that I would face time and time again:

Is this a person who was psychotic before drugs?

Is this a person who is psychotic because they are on drugs?

Is this a person who will be psychotic after drugs?

It was often impossible to unpick the cause and effect and the task was made more problematic by the fact that most of the buggers would never give an honest answer.

"Are you sure you're not using drugs, Terry?"

Terry was sweating profusely, had pupils the size of watermelons and dried blood caked around his septum.

"No!" he said, outraged at such a suggestion.

"Because it's okay if you are," I continued, "we can

look at how to reduce it over time and think about how to keep you safe."

But he maintained he had not used.

As I drove away from his house I received a text.

Bring me 3g coke and 2 cans Monster ta.

It was from Terry.

I texted him back.

Hi Terry –was that last text meant for me?

He didn't reply.

As someone trying to help those people affected by substance misuse, I was usually on the periphery of the drug scene. This was to change when I took Lee, a four-foot-tall terror who had become unwell at Glastonbury and thought Neil Diamond was the devil, to his doctor's appointment.

The appointment went without incident and he was advised to take prescribed legal drugs (that made him fat, dribble and lethargic) and avoid illegal drugs (that made him feel like the king of the world).

I wasn't optimistic of the chances of him following this advice.

On the drive back Lee politely asked if I could stop off at one of his friends which I duly did. We carried on and, five minutes later, he asked if I could stop at another friend's house. Always trying to improve the therapeutic relationship, I agreed. At the third house my suspicions were growing and by the fourth house, when I saw him walking towards my car folding a bundle of £10 notes, the penny dropped.

"Are you selling drugs?" I demanded as he sat in the car

"No," he said defensively. My eyes bore into him. "Well…"

"Lee!"

I couldn't believe it.

I was a social worker – I listened to Gardeners' Question Time, was a member of the National Trust and had a plastic cover to stop my banana being bruised…

And here I was, a wheel man doing drug runs for Mr Big (well, Mr Small).

Luckily I had an ally in my war on drugs: Ken. Ken was a support worker with a local charity and worked with many of my trickiest customers. A high tolerance to risk and a personal history that featured drugs, alcohol, violence and imprisonment meant that he was perfectly placed to engage with the little fuckers that I sent his way:

An aggressive homeless man that no one else would touch – Ken would throw him in the back of his car and take them to the council.

A psychotic twenty-year-old waking up with heroin withdrawal – Ken would bundle them in front of their GP.

A young man who had severed his own foreskin with a potato peeler – Ken would have him at his badminton club by lunchtime.

In fact, Ken had everyone at his badminton club – young, old, able-bodied, significant physical disabilities, keen and motivated or strongly resisting; they all ended up at the badminton group.

Unlike traditional badminton groups, Ken's badminton group differed slightly in the fact that, as far as I was aware, no one ever played badminton. Instead they would stand, smoke and swear outside the main reception, hoping that being in the close vicinity of a leisure centre would be enough to get them fit. Only once did I take someone who showed any interest in actually playing a game of badminton and, when I returned several hours later I found him, having been unable to secure an opponent, hitting a shuttlecock over the net and running round the other side to hit it back to himself. The total lack of badminton at Ken's badminton group was best typified by an incident I saw with one member who had been every week for over three years.

"What's this Ken?" he asked, picking up an object from the floor and regarding it with puzzlement.

It was a shuttlecock.

Time after time I would see how these drug-taking, high risk youths would casually dismiss my cautious, Radio 4-listening, stately home visiting, banana-protecting approach, but idolise Ken, a father figure who had always done much worse than them.

"I'm looking at three months in prison," wept one of our young drug dealers.

"Three months?" said Ken disparagingly, "half that for good behaviour and you'll be out in six weeks – we called that a shit and a shower, mate."

Or, on learning that one of his young charges was caning £50 of coke each morning, Ken would be singularly unimpressed. Cradling their head in his hands like the Pope ready to anoint, he would peer up their nasal cavity.

"You need to flush this or you're going to end up like me. Every time I catch a cold my sinuses blow up like a balloon. Thirty years of fucking agony."

I could see the fear in the boy's eyes as he vowed never to snort again (he went on to inject).

And through it all, Ken showed levels of compassion

to these whippersnappers that frequently put me to shame. I was run ragged dealing with the crimewave that they generated, and I was not averse to the odd prison sentence here and there to give me a bit of respite.

But Ken would do everything in his power to keep them out of jail.

At the end of the trial of Eddie who in the previous months had been arrested for drunk and disorderly three times, found in possession of numerous offensive weapons and had tried to break into the local police station twice, Ken phoned me.

"He's got off!" he said happily, "the judge read my report and what I'd arranged with the probation officer and only gave him community service!"

"That's great news," I said, slumping onto my desk.

Ken drove a rusty Corsa that had had so many repairs there were only trace elements of the original car remaining and he had to hotwire it every time he wanted to get it started. When he bought it, the radio didn't work and it had one CD jammed into it on perpetual play.

Ken loved classical music, Irish folk and baroque.

The CD was Body Count by Ice T.

One day I was following him on a visit to a bail hostel that I had never been to before but had heard lots of bad things about.

He pulled up outside a rundown building.

"It's a real shithole, isn't it?" I said, following him up the path.

"This is my house, you cheeky bastard! I was just popping in to pick up my sandwiches."

Ken's deep understanding of the streets was matched only by his vast knowledge of literature and I was always impressed by his ability to produce a quote for every situation we faced together.

A man hysterically telling us that the child his girlfriend was carrying was not his was treated to some Mark Twain:

"Forgiveness is the fragrance that the violet sheds on the heel that has crushed it."

"That may be so, Ken, but she shagged my best mate!"

A woman in the midst of a gender identity crisis got Wilde:

"Be yourself for everyone else is taken."

"I don't want to be my fookin' self, Ken, that's the point!"

And, when a group of us were out on a day's rock-climbing and I realised that the person holding my safety rope was smoking a joint, Ken consoled me with some Hemingway:

"The best way to find out if you trust somebody is to trust them," (though I'm willing to bet that Ernest wasn't two hundred feet up on a tiny rocky outcrop, with his life in the hands of a teenager tooting on ganja when he came up with that one).

Frustrated with my inability to help people like Terry, Lee and Eddie I eventually signed myself up for a crash course in Motivational Interviewing; an approach which provided practitioners with the skills to enable people to identify unwanted behaviours in their lives and influence them to change.

It was a sneaky form of counselling; a Jedi Mind trick for addicts.

"These aren't the cans of Stella you are looking for."

"These aren't the cans of Stella I am looking for."

I was keen for the course to be a success but was

immediately put on the back foot when I saw my name on the computer-generated list of attendees and realised that, having completed the online enrolment with an overly sensitive mouse, I had managed to put my title as Archdeacon rather than Mr.

The course started by going through the fundamentals of the approach and, despite being told that this was central to its successful application, I soon drifted off, imaging all the nefarious ways in which I could misuse my newly-acquired powers to subliminally influence the actions of others. When I eventually came to, everyone else seemed to know what they were doing and I had to spend the next three days trying not to make eye contact when they were looking for volunteers and going for long toilet breaks when I could see a group discussion looming over the horizon.

By the end of the final day I could only remember two things.

Dance the dance! (I had no idea what this meant but our fanatical facilitator would shout it every few minutes) and The Cycle of Change. The Cycle of Change identified the stages people would go through before change could be affected and comprised of the pre-contemplative stage (no intention of changing behaviour), contemplative (aware problem exists but with no commitment to action), preparation (intent on taking action to address the problem) and, finally, action (active modification of unwanted behaviour). It was a relatively straightforward concept to grasp and, as we filtered out of the hall, I was eager to try and apply it to my practice as soon as possible.

The next morning I was at Terry's house, brimming with enthusiasm and banging on his front door. After twenty minutes, he stumbled downstairs and opened it, wiping sleep from his eyes and irritably pulling his boxer shorts out of his bum crack.

"What do you want?" he growled.

(Pre-contemplative.)

"I wondered if we could have a chat about how things are going?"

"Urghhh."

(Contemplative.)

"It won't take long," I assured him.

"Can we not do it later?"

(Preparation.)

I channelled my training. "No, let's dance the dance now."

"Get to fuck," he said, slamming the door in my face.

(Action.)

THIRTY-FIVE

Unimpressed by the general lack of resources available for carers, I decided that I would start a group for the friends and families of people who used our service. This would give them the opportunity to come and share their experiences, listen to the struggles of others and go home with the warm feeling that there was somebody in an even worse situation than them.

I decided to launch this venture with a regular evening meeting and, to take some of the pressure off me, I invited a different guest speaker each week to talk about a particular theme. My colleagues had fed back that there was a lot of interest for the event and provided me with long lists of people who said that they would be coming. I booked a large hall in the centre of town and sent out several hundred invites. When the first night arrived, I decided to set out just fifty seats so that there would be no chance of empty spaces – besides, there were stacks of chairs at the back of the hall and standing room if these weren't enough. I hired a projector, printed off a pile of handouts and spent a considerable amount of my own money on high quality biscuits that I laid out on plates, alongside tea, coffee and hot chocolate.

Three people came.

Of these, one was a young woman on my caseload who I didn't have the heart to tell she shouldn't be there (and had to spend successive weeks watching her eat her own body weight in my Viennese Whirls) and the other two were a husband and wife whose son had gone to live on a kibbutz two years earlier.

Once it became clear that no one else was going to arrive, I stood up in front of the forty-seven empty seats and thanked everyone for coming, aware that tonight's guest speaker, an experienced and much respected mindfulness instructor, was currently lugging a gong across town expecting to find a large, enthusiastic crowd waiting for him.

As I finished my introduction he came in, sweating profusely and looking around in puzzlement.

"Oh sorry," he apologised, turning to leave, "I think I must have the wrong place."

I leapt over to him and explained that he was in the right place and I had expected a much bigger turnout and could he please, please stay or I would have to talk on my own for the next two hours. Eventually he agreed and I spent the next forty-five minutes silently trying to achieve inner harmony whilst someone behind me started to make inroads into the Bourbon Creams.

The following week I turned to drugs and alcohol or, more specifically, how best to support people who were abusing them. This drew a much larger crowd and, as Duncan the specialist worker took to the podium, five people sat listening intently.

I looked at their faces, exhausted by the unconditional support that they had given to their loved ones as they battled through the ravages of addiction.

They had come here tonight because they had nowhere else to turn, nothing left to cling on to.

They looked to Duncan for help.

They looked to Duncan for hope.

"I don't believe in rock bottom," said Duncan, as he put up a slide of a sclerotic liver, "too many people I know have sailed right through it and are now lying cold in the cemetery."

In an attempt to try and make things a bit more uplifting I decided that the next meeting would focus upon the Recovery model; an approach in mental health which emphasised hope, optimism and positive outcomes. The audience continued to grow (eight) and there was a relaxed atmosphere as the speaker, an older peer-specialist within the Recovery movement, mingled amongst them.

"Shall we make a circle of chairs?" she suggested, after everyone had got a drink, "I find the stage a bit too corporate."

There were murmurs of agreement and disapproving glances towards me and my podium. I helped move the chairs, surreptitiously pulling my shirt out of my trousers and tousling my hair to try and look a bit more groovy.

"That's better," she continued, "I feel less like a performing monkey. Now, the Recovery model has given me a future, it's allowed me to dream, it's given me the tools I need to move forward with my life…"

Finally, I thought, something positive for the carers to hold on to.

Something to give them energy.

Something to provide them with reassurance.

Something to enable them to face tomorrow with a renewed sense of hope.

"…but it's taken me well over thirty of years of hell, despair and anguish to get here," she finished.

Despite the handful of people who attended leaving more depressed than when they arrived, I was encouraged to continue running the carer's group by my manager because it was one of eight government targets that the service was required to meet. Amongst the other targets were Family Intervention, vocational support and an annual physical health check.

As employees of a health service we were expected to carry out the annual
physical health checks ourselves and, whilst my nurse colleagues set about the task with gusto I, a social worker who could barely touch a raw chicken drumstick, struggled. The pressure to meet these targets was great since they were linked to the amount of funding the service received and each month a spreadsheet would be circulated showing which workers met or missed the targets. Shamed by the sea of red that would routinely be next to my name, I decided to sign myself up to the physical health check training.

In preparation for the course I had to have access to a range of equipment including scales, tape measure, stethoscope, thermometer and sphygmomanometer.

I went to my manager to request these.

"I gave you those last year," she said, "you put them in the boot of your car."

I had no recollection of this but went to check my car just to be sure.

My manager followed.

"There," she said, pointing to a large black canvas bag that was taking up three quarters of my boot space.

"Oh," I said, unzipping it to find scales, tape measure, stethoscope, thermometer and sphygmomanometer inside.

Having forgotten that I had put it in my boot, I had later assumed that the bag must have come with the car and contained a hazard triangle, fluorescent jackets and jump leads. I had even transferred it over to our other car when we had travelled around Europe earlier in the year in case we had a breakdown.

The physical health training course involved two long days of cholesterol levels, glucose readings, systolic and diastolic blood pressures, sinoatrial nodes and arrhythmia. The tutor was highly experienced, deeply knowledgeable and a skilled communicator but she may as well have delivered the training in her native Urdu for all the sense it made to me. At the end of the day we were given a practical examination in which we were marked on our ability to carry out the checks on each other. Under the watchful eye of the unimpressed tutor, I repeatedly took the pulse rate of my own thumb rather than the patient and several of the readings that I did manage were consistent with those of a person who was clinically dead. She finally asked me to stop when I pumped up the inflatable cuff of the blood pressure machine so tight that the person's arm went blue and they lost all feeling in their fingers.

With the annual physical health check covered, I turned my attention to the next target: Family Intervention. In order to meet this requirement, members of the team would go out in pairs and, over the course of several months, provide information, advice and support to all those involved with (and including) the person who used our service. I had done Family Intervention training the previous year and found that it suited my style of work. Unlike other therapies I had experienced, which ranged from nebulous chit chats to sinister mind control, Family Intervention work was structured, direct and honest. We would meet with everybody involved, identify common problems and work towards finding the best solutions.

My first opportunity to undertake Family Intervention was with Natasha and her parents. My colleague and I arrived at the house and, as we approached the door, we were both cacking it.

"They're very nice," I said with a quivering voice, "and at least there's only the three of them."

Her mum answered and showed us into the dining room.

Nine people sat around a table looking at us expectantly.

My first thought was to run. My second thought was why weren't these bastards at the carers group? We introduced ourselves to the assorted brothers, sisters, cousins, aunts and uncles.

"And there's Granny Edna," said Mum pointing at a television behind me.

"Hello," said Granny Edna, who was Skyping from New Zealand in her nightie.

After our initial assessment of the family, it became clear that the main difficulty was a lack of understanding about the impact that Natasha's mental health problems were having upon her. They mistook her lack of energy and motivation for laziness and felt that her withdrawal into her bedroom was a choice rather than a necessity.

Over the following weeks we looked at the symptoms of her illness in detail, focussing on the detrimental effects it could have upon social functioning. We discussed the importance of creating a supportive environment, seeking to avoid pressure and stress wherever possible.

We talked about emphasising any achievements rather than focussing upon the negatives, of identifying small goals that over time could be achieved.

"So," I said, confident that we had ushered in a new climate of tolerance and understanding towards Natasha, "where do we go from here?"

There was a short pause.

"She needs to go to college," said her mum.

"Or get a full-time job," said her dad.

"She should go the gym," said her sister.

"And try internet dating," said her brother

"She should do them all," chipped in Granny Edna, "as soon as possible!"

Natasha held her head in her hands.

It was well understood that regular work, be it paid or voluntary, improved self-esteem, confidence and overall mental wellbeing (unless you were a dentist or farmer, in which case it improved your chances of hanging yourself) and so the government had identified vocational support as another key target for our service. After getting to know Sandra, a woman who had come to the attention of services after she had submitted a mixed media portrait of Mussolini into her local village show, it was clear that spending long days alone doodling fascist dictators was doing her no favours and so I decided to take her to a local charity shop which was advertising for volunteers.

As well as wanting to break the negative cycle that she

was stuck in, I was also keen to make amends with Sandra as, when I first met her, I was in a phase of recommending to everyone I worked with a powerful book I had read about a person's experience of mental health.

"It's called The Unquiet One and you must read it," I had enthused and Sandra, like many other people before her, had promptly rushed out to buy it.

Unfortunately, it later transpired that the book that I had read which detailed a woman's courageous battle with bipolar disorder was An Unquiet Mind rather than The Unquiet One which was an in-depth history of the Pakistani national cricket team.

As we approached the shop together, Sandra tried to turn around but I managed to persuade her to go in. Once inside, we went to the counter, explained why we were there and were given an application form by the kindly assistant.

We decided to complete it straight away.

The charity was the RSPCA and we carefully wrote down Sandra's past experience, qualifications and why she wanted to do the job. When we reached the section on criminal convictions, she flushed.

"Do you have anything to declare Sandra?" I asked gently.

She remained quiet.

"Don't worry love," said the woman, "it doesn't mean you can't work here."

"Come on, let's just put it down," I coaxed, "what was it for?"

"I got a suspended sentence six months ago for animal cruelty."

THIRTY-SIX

Every two minutes in England a child is born, a train is cancelled and a 'once in a generation' service redesign takes place within the NHS. So when my manager left the team in order to take up a less stressful job (bomb disposal) and I was told that a review of the whole service would take place, I paid little notice.

When I was interviewed by a management consultant about my role I barely raised an eyebrow.

When I was asked to complete an audit of my work I filled it in without interest.

But when I was told that, due to reductions in government funding, my manager would not be replaced, my other manager's post would be lost, the caseload would be increased and our catchment area doubled, my interest was piqued.

My initial response to this news was a mild anxiety.

My colleagues' response was to flee.

As soon as possible.

There were so many leaving collections over such short a period of time that I am still unable to pass a brown envelope without popping a pound in it. Within months I was the only surviving member of a once thriving team. Seven people had left and I was the last one standing. I felt like the woman from The Hunger Games.

I struggled on seeing the people on my caseload but had

none of the usual support systems around me. There was no local team meeting, no supervision, no colleagues to bounce ideas off.

I was lost to the system.

I became feral.

Each morning I would turn on my laptop, expecting news of a disaster that I knew was coming. It seemed a matter of when, not if. I stopped sleeping, developed a twitch in my right eyelid, became anxious in crowded places and fearful when alone. I was preoccupied with work, on one occasion asking my young daughter to hush up whilst I tried to pick up an answer machine message only to realise after that she had been choking on a Wotsit.

To try and counter my stress and make myself a bit more bearable to those around me, I took out a membership at my local swimming pool but, on the one occasion in months that I managed to go, I calculated that each lap had cost me £45. Although others could see the impact my work was having upon me, I had little insight and, having become aware that each Monday morning I would awake with a sore tummy, I went to see my GP to find the cause.

"Tell me straight Dr Tomkins, is it cancer?"

"No, its mild anxiety," he replied (a little too straight, I felt).

There were some minor advantages to being the last remaining member of the team. It gave me flexibility in the hours that I worked, I was able to make decisions independently and Secret Santa became much more simple (which, considering that in the last Secret Santa I was involved in I was given a raw pig's trotter with varnished nails, was not inconsequential).

But I knew that when the tragedy occurred (and it would occur) then I would really be in the shit. What I needed was a period of calm until the staffing situation could be resolved.

It never came.

Near miss after near miss followed, each one more terrifying than the last.

It started with Liz, who had gone on holiday on a cruise ship. Several days in I received a call from one of the staff on board.

"Jumped in…" I managed to pick out on the crackly line, "Unable to reach her…inform her next of kin…"

The line went dead.

After many frantic international calls, I was able to track down the member of staff and find out exactly what had happened.

On becoming distressed by the comments of another passenger, Liz had run at full pelt along the length of the deck shouting, There's no place like home! There's no place like home! before jumping into the ship's swimming pool.

I was relieved to discover that, rather than the Atlantic Ocean, as I had first feared, she had only dive bombed into the middle of an aqua aerobics session.

Arthur lived with his mum and, at one of our initial meetings, told me that he was thinking about killing himself.

"And have you thought how you'd do this?" I asked.

"Hang myself in the garage," he said, with the type of nonchalance that made you sit up and pay attention. We explored this at length and after pinning him down on some protective factors (primarily his love of his mum and boxing) I felt it was okay to leave him at home overnight.

I returned the next morning

"Is Arthur about?" I asked his mum.

"He's in the garage," she replied, "which is odd because he never usually goes in there this early and he's been in there for hours."

As I slowly pushed the door open I heard it immediately; the unmistakable sound of something heavy swinging on a rope.

Feeling sick, and against all my natural instincts, I forced myself to look in.

"Oh hello!" said Arthur, giving his punch bag one final uppercut.

Vanessa loved the outdoors and had decided to go on a walking holiday.

"The Cotswolds?" I asked.

"Kilimanjaro," she joked and we both laughed.

The day before she was due to go away I popped in to see her. I walked into her front room to find all manner of ice picks, helmets, webbing, flares and ropes spread across the carpet.

She was going to Kilimanjaro.

"Have you done this sort of thing before?" I asked nervously.

"Never," she replied, rolling up an oxygen mask.

Over the following weeks, every time my phone rang I expected it to be the Tanzanian emergency services asking me to come and identify a frozen figure in crampons, but no call came and Vanessa eventually returned home safely (albeit with first degree sunburn, amoebic dysentery and a selfie of her and an alpaca balanced precariously on the edge of a mile-deep crevice).

The nearest of near misses during this time was performed by Seema Khan who I saw (when she chose to answer the door) to try and talk about her mental health, but always ended up discussing gardening, politics and Game of Thrones. At the end of our last meeting, Seema thanked me for coming, showed me out of the door and tried to jump off the roof. Her husband, who was peering out of the attic window because he thought he could hear a squirrel fiddling with the satellite dish, managed to grab her and pull her inside.

Half an hour later I was back at his house.

"Why didn't you say how you were feeling?" I asked as I tried to arrange a hospital admission and calm her badly shaken family.

"It didn't seem that important," she shrugged.

We had spoken at length about the best plants for shaded areas, proportional representation and whether Daenerys Stormborn of the House Targaryen, Khaleesi of the Great Grass Sea and Breaker of Chains had been in Coronation Street, but she didn't think it was relevant to tell me that she intended to jump off the roof the minute I was out of the door.

Months passed, seasons changed and the staffing situation remained critical. I roamed the countryside, appearing at people's houses to warn them about the dangers of isolation without having seen another colleague myself in weeks. My car was full of paperwork and old food, I ate in hard shoulders and urinated in bushes (after checking there were no primary school children nearby). My feeling of being lost in the system was reinforced by my wage slips which gave me a different job title each month.

Psychologist.

Nurse.

Cleaner.

Mother of Dragons.

It didn't help my sense of identity and it didn't help my mortgage application.

When I surfaced at teams, people looked at me with vague recognition.

"Are you the book club man?" they would ask.

"What's happening with your team?" a nurse inquired one day.

"They've done a big recruitment campaign but have only had one applicant," I replied.

"And what's the job like?" she asked.

"There's no supervision, no team meetings, no support, high caseloads and high risk cases."

"God, it sounds terrible."

"It is, but let's hope the applicant doesn't find out."

She stood looking awkward.

"You're the applicant aren't you," I said.

She was and she promptly withdrew her application.

When I was able to access my emails I received a stream

of jolly updates from my colleagues who had left the service.

The new team's great, today we had some really helpful team development sessions and tomorrow evening we're all going out for a meal!

I've only got six people on my caseload which means I can really make a difference to their lives!

Things are so quiet here I'm actually bored!

These emails would be interspersed with messages about my own work.

Eddie has been arrested for trying to break into a police station again.

Mr Khan has phoned to say there's something on the roof and it's too big to be a squirrel.

Could you contact the Tanzanian emergency services immediately.

Ken was still about and we tried our best to carry on, arranging regular group events to try and see as many people as possible with minimal effort.

We started a photography group which, in keeping with our badminton philosophy, did very little photography. Mindful of my tendency to set the agenda, we agreed that the venues would be chose by the group and so, for our first week, Andre chose an abandoned farm.

"Are you sure this is abandoned?" I asked as we climbed over a padlocked gate.

"No one's been here for years," he assured me.

So why is there fresh hay? I pondered.

Why is there steaming manure?

Why is there a farmer with a shotgun coming across the field?

Over the next weeks, Andre took us to an uninhabited

haunted house (inhabited), a disused train track (used) and an unoccupied army barracks (occupied) before we asked another member to decide future venues.

Out of every activity we tried, paintballing was by far the most popular. Swathed in tightly-fitting boiler suits, Ken and I would sidle into the woods whilst fifteen young people, honed in the art of warfare by countless hours in front of Call of Duty, would hunt us down like dogs. At our first paintballing day out, we were blissfully unaware of the pain that those little balls of brightly coloured paint could cause and, opting for a flanking movement, we casually strolled along the edges of the woods.

They got Ken first.

I heard his squeals of agony as his hands, legs, back and ears were peppered with shots.

He cried for my help.

I promptly dived into some nearby undergrowth and spent the rest of the game trembling amongst the ferns, listening to Ken's occasional screams and wondering how I could get away from all of this.

THIRTY-SEVEN

"It's an area that I feel I have a good knowledge of," I told the panel who were interviewing me for a post with the perinatal service.

Ten minutes earlier I had been frantically calling my wife from the waiting room. "How long's a woman pregnant for?" I whispered, aware that this was something I should probably know when applying to work exclusively with pregnant women.

My wife had laughed initially but when it became clear I was serious she was far from impressed. As the mother of my three children she felt it highlighted a lack of attention to detail. Thank goodness I hadn't asked her my original query about where, exactly, did the baby come out from.

Luckily, gestation and anatomy never arose and, by emphasising my previous experience of working with pregnant women (which consisted of being chased around a flat in the dark by someone who wanted to run me through with a sink plunger) I was given the job. Whilst I was thankful to be leaving my old post I dreaded having to tell the people on my caseload that I would be going. Usually another worker would be identified and you would all meet together to ensure a smooth transfer took place. But with a job that was less appealing than haemorrhoids, I knew that there would be no one in post to hand over to and so I set about saying my goodbyes and trying to cobble together some form of plan for everyone I worked with.

I was determined not to make false promises about keeping in touch because, over the course of my career, I had seen my departing colleagues break promises time and time again and I resolved to be honest and upfront.

Sitting down with Terry, someone I'd helped negotiate numerous difficulties over the years, my stomach flipped with nerves.

"I'm really sorry to tell you this Terry, but…with one thing or another I'm…not able to continue with this job and so…I'm going to…have to…leave."

With tears welling up, I avoided eye contact in case I set him off as well.

"Thank fuck for that," he said before resuming Grand Theft Auto.

Other people were less accepting.

"If I get pregnant can we still work together?" asked Seema.

I explained that this would probably not be a good idea and besides, in all the times I'd been to her house she'd only opened the door on a few occasions and the last of those had ended with her trying to throw herself off the roof. But I was aware that, for some people, having a worker in the background, even if they only saw them occasionally to complete a job application, apply for housing or drive them around selling cocaine, was a safety net that allowed them to move forward with confidence. And people knew that in the current climate of cuts to health and social care they might not be reallocated a worker in the future. The political impetus was now for measurable, tidy, time-limited interventions – six sessions of Cognitive

Behavioural Therapy, an eLearning anxiety management package, a Donnie Darko DVD – none of which, I felt, was a substitute for a good working relationship with someone you trusted.

Yet on I pressed, meeting with everybody on my caseload and, for every person who saw this as an opportunity to move towards recovery and thanking me for my help, another would throw a television at me. Kim wondered whether she could now be rude to me if she saw me in town. Since she had spent the last year cruelly mocking my receding hairline, taste in music and fashion sense, I could only imagine what she had planned.

Marcus bought me a carefully wrapped present which touched me deeply until I opened it and saw it was a guide to developing better people skills. Alice, to whom I had laid myself bare by showing her some of my writing, bought me a book on how to write better. People who had little gave me all sorts of gifts and, as I approached my final day, my car was laden with boxes of chocolates, bottles of wine, a small bag of crack and a life-size papier-mâché giraffe's head (and neck).

The last person I had to tell was Ken and I worried about what this would do to him. As well as the groups, we had both become entangled in a very messy case where the young woman we were working with was, like many others we worked with, a drug dealer. What made this case special was that it was on an industrial scale and involved the whole family, from her little nephew to her great grandma. Everyone was involved. It was like the Colombian Waltons.

Early on, Ken and I had decided that, rather than report them to the police, we were going to focus on trying to improve the young woman's mental health. Although ignoring the ongoing illegal activities was against our service policy, it was our belief that recovery rather than prison would be best for her. And her Auntie Janice not hunting us down with a pack of Pitbull terriers would be best for us.

At first, turning a blind eye was simple. We would look away when we saw measuring scales on the dining table or boxes of baggies on the floor. But as the family became more comfortable with us they gradually let their guard down. As Ken and I talked about the potential benefits of a college course, there would be a knock at the door and several dangerous-looking men would be given packages by Uncle Peter. Our session on Early Warning Signs was interrupted by her niece, Becky, serving up wraps of coke to a steady stream of pasty-faced youths. And when, during Ken's traditional hard sell of the badminton group, Grandpa Tony brushed past us with a shotgun, we knew things were out of control.

It was clear that I could not leave Ken alone with this and needed to discharge the young woman before I changed jobs.

The only question was how.

There were various routes for being discharged from our service, including death and going to prison. Both of these were distinct possibilities but, as we were still not willing to snitch and I was not prepared to murder (Ken did not dismiss the idea entirely), this could take some time. As I struggled to think of other options available, I received a call from the young woman to ask if I could come and see her. After negotiating the electric fence, moat, drawbridge and fortified front door, she invited me in and told me that the family had decided to move out of the area. Whilst I remained concerned about her mental health (during the meeting she had told Ken that she would never use drugs again – this was concerning as Ken wasn't there) there was little more I could do than pass on all the relevant information to the team that served the area that her family would soon be moving (and dealing) to.

With everyone told, I attended my final badminton group where I was able to meet up with many of the people I had spent the last few years working with to say a final farewell. As we stood, smoked and swore (but not play badminton), I felt tremendously lucky that I had joined a profession that gave me the chance to get to know these individuals and try and make a positive impact upon their lives.

Sometimes this happened, often it did not.

But it still felt a privilege.

*

The next day I set off to begin my new job, my mind racing, my car washed, my cardigan ironed. Just like at the train station, twenty years earlier, I was nervous about what was waiting for me but excited about the possibilities. A host of people and situations I had yet to encounter were in the distance and I sped happily towards them.

Until I got stuck behind a tractor.

AFTERWORD

In the twenty-five years since I stood at the train station, about to take my first tentative steps into the world of health and social care, six people that I have worked with have threatened to kill me, two have actively tried, one has kicked me in the seat of my pants, three have made formal complaints about me (one directly to the Prime Minister), three have tried to covertly medicate me and two people have put curses upon me (one voodoo, one gypsy). I have had to attend countless training courses, sit through all manner of meetings, fill in innumerable forms and endure a pay freeze longer than other people's careers.

And yet...

Last month I was able to introduce two people to each other who thought that they were the only ones that felt the way they did.

Last week I got to spend half an hour playing animal dominoes with the three-year-old daughter of a person I had just started to work with.

Yesterday I laughed so hard in a team meeting that I accidentally snotted into my tea.

Today someone told me about worries that they have kept secret for years.

Tomorrow ...